Introduction to Christianity
A Case Method Approach

INTRODUCTION TO
CHRISTIANITY
A CASE METHOD
APPROACH

ALICE F. EVANS
and
ROBERT A. EVANS

John Knox Press
ATLANTA

Scripture quotations from the Revised Standard Version of the Holy Bible, copyright, 1946, 1952, and © 1971, 1973 by the Division of Christian Education, National Council of the Churches of Christ in the U.S.A. and used by permission.

Excerpts from *The Jerusalem Bible*, copyright © 1966 by Darton, Longman & Todd, Ltd. and Doubleday & Company, Inc. Used by permission of the publisher.

Library of Congress Cataloging in Publication Data
Evans, Robert A   1937–
   Introduction to Christianity.

   Bibliography: p.
   1. Christianity—Essence, genius, nature.
I. Evans, Alice F., 1939–   joint author.
II. Title.
BT60.E9   209   79-87752
ISBN 0-8042-1314-3

10 9 8 7 6 5 4 3 2 1
© copyright 1980 John Knox Press
Printed in the United States of America
Atlanta, Georgia 30308

Dedication:

To Mommilee and Faddy;
Mother and Aunt Dorothy:
Instructors in Life and Faith

Preface

WHO AM I?

WHAT DO I VALUE?

WHY AM I HERE?

WHERE AM I GOING?

The 1977 TV series based on *Roots,* (N.Y.: Doubleday, 1976) Alex Haley's novel about a black American family's pursuit of freedom, was watched by more Americans than any other show in the history of entertainment. The book *Passages* (N.Y.: E. P. Dutton, 1976) by Gail Sheehy, describing crises in adult life, has been a number one national non-fiction best seller. This kind of national response indicates that questions about the importance and meaning of life, about what we value, and how we act on these commitments are important for a large number of people. However, from age fourteen to twenty-two, the high school and college years, the concerns about "Who is the real me?" and "What do I want from parents, friends, or even myself?" sometimes take on crisis quality.

Christianity, like other great religions of the world, responds to these questions as it influences how we think, feel, and act. Even when we are unaware of it, we often are affected by many of the basic ideas of Christianity which have become so much a part of our American culture. Many Christians believe that their religion also contains guidelines for living a full life with both responsibility and freedom. Jesus, the central figure in Christianity, declares he lived so that we might be able to experience life in all its fullness. The problem which faces us at any age is, "What does it mean to live fully?" Parents and children, friends and enemies, even the world's great religions disagree about the best way to answer this question. Throughout our lives we are faced with situations which seem to force us to choose between being "free" and being "responsible," between accepting or rejecting a person or an idea, or even between life and death. If you are asked to lie to one friend to protect a promise made to another friend, you will hurt one of your friends. How do you decide? If a friend is faced with an unwanted pregnancy, would you recommend an abortion? Why or why not? Christians do not believe that their faith dictates specifically what to do in every situation, but they do believe that it offers keys or guidelines for making decisions about the ordinary as well as crisis events of human life. For this decision-making Christians draw on the resources or stories of their own experiences: on their special book—the Bible; on their special history—tradition; on their special beliefs—doctrine; and on their special celebrations—ritual.

For several years "value clarification" has been an important topic in many schools. But Christianity is more concerned about value "formation" than about value "clarification." Christians believe that not only *why* you make an ethical decision but *which* decision you make will be reflected in the story of your life. Other views of the world—Humanism, Islam, Buddhism—may offer alternative choices and reasons. The authors respect these differences. Yet the purpose of this book is to help interested persons learn and evaluate what many Christians believe and how they seek to act. We have found that some of the most honest, open, and concerned persons we know are teenagers and young adults. So this book was written for and with teenagers and their parents, young adults and their elders. It is in a dialogue between the generations that differences in commitments and beliefs may test why and whether we are living life as fully as possible. This exercise for understanding the effect of Christian beliefs on decision-making is prepared for use in schools and colleges, for discussion groups and classes in churches of all denominations, for young people and adults, and for persons who want a brief introduction to the main concerns of the Christian religion.

It is these students, young and old, who have turned out to be our most important instructors. In testing this volume with college and graduate students, over two hundred juniors and seniors in four different high schools—inner-city and suburban, private and parochial—we had our belief confirmed that the study of Christianity can be exciting and relevant. We have shared this material in churches of many denominations, community groups of all sizes, and in organizations from teen clubs to the U.S. Navy. These discussions were greatly facilitated by the case method and the initially cautious and then enthusiastic participation of students in this approach to learning based on experience. The text was radically revised, and we trust substantively improved, as a result of the systematic and thorough evaluation of this material by students, teachers, parents, and parishioners involved in the project.

We wish to express our gratitude to all those in schools, colleges, churches and clubs, whether willing or unwilling participants, from whom we learned so much. To the leaders and teachers who became co-learners in this project, often facing controversial issues in their teaching, we are also indebted—for their time, the frustration of helping develop a new method, and the creative suggestions which emerged from their constructive and critical reviews. The authors' thanks go especially to: Howard Feddema, Social Studies Department of Arlington Heights Township High School; Sally Cummins, Religion Department of Mother Guerin Roman Catholic High School; Bill Bertsche, History Department of The Latin School of Chicago; Nancy Kolos, J. McCormick, and T. Tomczyk of Thomas Kelly High School; the administrators of these greater Chicago area schools; and the Chicago Board of Education which granted permission to field test this material and to the persons too numerous to name in churches and community organizations across the U.S. who helped create this book.

The authors have used the Bible as a "working companion" throughout this volume. Important biblical passages are often quoted directly in the text. Other passages which are too lengthy to quote or are referred to primarily for confirmation of an idea are simply cited for the reader's further reference. In either case the scripture reference is given in the same general form, i.e. Matthew 19:19 RSV. This refers to the book of Matthew, the nineteenth chapter, and the nineteenth verse from the Revised Standard Version of the Bible. It is not so important for the purposes of this study which of the many translations of the Bible a reader selects; various Christian traditions recognize different translations. In seeking to respect these traditions, the authors have alternated the use of five principal translations. Our aim was to select the text with the clearest English meaning and to expose the reader to translations of the Bible that have greatly influenced the shape of our language. The following initials indicate the translations employed:

DB = Douay Bible; JB = Jerusalem Bible; KJV = King James Version; NEB = New English Bible; and RSV = Revised Standard Version.

Due to anticipated use in public and private schools at the college and high school level, this volume has sought to follow the basic guidelines for the teaching of religion in public schools as set out by the Schempp decision of the Supreme Court (1963). This decision encourages the "objective *study* of" or "teaching *about*" religion as necessary for a complete education. At the same time, the decision prohibits the *practice* of religion (in the form of prayer or devotional Bible reading) which would constitute the study *of* religion. The authors consulted with persons who are recognized authorities on the teaching of religion in public education before they undertook any writing on the volume. We wish to express appreciation to those who shared generously their experience, time, creative suggestions, and warnings. Our gratitude goes especially to: Rodney F. Allen, Edwin S. Gaustad, Thomas Love, Robert Michaelsen, C. Ellis Nelson, Robert A. Spivey, Leon Weinberger, and to two members of The Public Education Religion Studies Center, James Panoch and Nicholas Piediscalz. Our thanks also go to many others with whom we had briefer encounters.

It is, of course, an impossible task to give a thorough presentation of Christianity, in all its diversity, within the scope of these few pages. Granted this limitation, the authors have attempted to make the study as adequate as possible and to check our own judgment with colleagues, particularly those representing other Christian traditions. Thus appropriate portions of the manuscript have been read by scholars in the Protestant, Eastern Orthodox, and Roman Catholic traditions, representing biblical studies, theology, and church history. To friends named here we express deep appreciation without holding them responsible for the final product: Professors Joseph A. Bracken S. J., Charles E. Carlston, Gabriel Fackre, Meredith B. Handspicker, William L. Holladay, Thomas D. Parker, Lewis Patsavos and Thomas A. Schafer. Also to colleagues in the Case-Study Institute, of which both authors are "Fellows," we acknowledge the enormous contribution made by the case method to whatever liveliness and relevance this volume may have.

Funds for initial stages of the research and for field testing were provided by the Cuesta Foundation of Tulsa, Oklahoma, for whose continued interest and support we are deeply grateful.

Appreciation for personal and technical support for projects like this is always inadequately expressed because this kind of assistance usually extends beyond the bounds of a particular endeavor. However, to colleagues and students at McCormick Theological Seminary, Hartford Seminary Foundation, and to the members of the Winnetka Presbyterian Church, many of whom were forced to encounter this material in different forms, we say thank you for patience, forbearance, constructive critique, and loving suppport. A special word to Lois Martin, Jan Jan Wong, Jeanne Holper, and Wilma Otte who typed endlessly and cheerfully for field testing or publication. Appreciation for editorial assistance on the text to Donald K. Swearer, Richard Ray, and to Gail and Wayne Russell. No words can encompass our debt to the family members to whom this work is dedicated.

Alice and Bob Evans
Simsbury, CT

CONTENTS

Introduction

Ted Lee brushed aside the long wet leaf on a banana plant that had just slapped him across the face with its dripping fingers. He wondered whether he could make it the last two hundred yards up the mountain in this sweltering heat and high grass, guided only by the flickering glow of the torches held to light his way. He was beginning to suspect that the decision to come to the Fiji Islands as a high school exchange student was a terrible mistake. From the moment he had gotten off the plane yesterday evening in Nadi, at the International Airport, after more than twenty hours on a flight from Chicago, he had been confused by a language he could not understand. He was not at all refreshed by a lunch of purple yams, roasted crayfish, and breadfruit. Even in the midst of the handsome, black young men who led him toward their home village in the hill country of the central island to be greeted by the elders of the clan, he was now feeling very isolated. In a few days he would travel on to his new home for a year in the capital city of Suva.

When Ted entered the village, everyone suddenly disappeared, and he felt even more anxious than before. Only later would he learn that he could not be recognized officially as "present" in the village until he had been welcomed by the village elders in the formal yagona ceremony. A few minutes later Ted sat cross-legged upon a grass mat in a bamboo-pole and thatch house; he was surrounded by the chanting village elders. Longi, Ted's seventeen-year-old Fijian host, sat at the very back of the room behind the elders. Ted suddenly realized that his confusion and anxiety must be what his U.S. advisor had described as "culture shock." One of the elders ceremoniously mixed the white powder of the kava root with water in a huge wooden bowl carved to represent a sea turtle. Ted then found himself being offered the first serving of the milky liquid in a cup made from half of a polished coconut shell. All eyes were on him. A gesture from his new host seemed to indicate he was to drink it all in one gulp. As Ted choked from the last of the chalky, bitter substance and held out the empty cup, a great deep "mmmm" came from the gathered local leaders. Had he done the wrong thing? Were they offended by his response? Everything was so strange!

After the elders had all drunk from the cup, Ted was escorted to another much larger Fijian dwelling called a *buri*, in which almost the entire village had gathered, seated on grass mats. As the people began to sing, he realized that this was a religious service of some kind. At that moment, he noticed what looked like a Bible on a low wooden table. Then Longi, who was to be Ted's translator, slipped up to his side and said, "Welcome to my home, and now yours, as we share the Lord's Supper together." It dawned on Ted that, in the midst of all the strange customs, clothes, and conditions that had encompassed him, here in a village in a distant area of the South Pacific, he was in the midst of a Christian service of worship. He could not yet understand the Fijian dialect into which the Bible verses used in this service had been translated; the elements of the communion service were not the traditional bread and wine served on silver trays, but juice from a local plant and a piece of cassava root which is a staple food; the *lali* drum beat out a tune he had never heard. Yet Ted saw the joy in the praises to God, addressed in a different tongue. He felt the concern of the leader of the service to help his people understand the power and message of the Bible. Ted realized that even though there were differences in language, climate, and location, he and these people shared a common commitment to the Christian faith; they were one people in God's sight.

Influence of Christianity.

Nearly one-fourth of the world's total population, approximately 984,000,000 persons, consider themselves Christians. These followers of the world's largest single religion differ in location, language, race, income, and even in the interpretation of the sacred literature of their religion, the Bible. However, there is a common affirmation that spans distance, time, and culture to bind them together. As a whole, the Christian community believes and proclaims " 'Jesus is Lord.' " (1 Corinthians 12:3 JB, NEB, RSV)

Christians believe that what God is like was "revealed" or shown to them in a special way through Jesus of Nazareth, a man born almost 2,000 years ago. Christians also believe that the way he lived, died, and overcame death can enable them to live life more fully. This is one way of interpreting Jesus' words, " 'I came that they might have life, and have it abundantly.' " (John 10:10 RSV) There are many persons who have every advantage in terms of food, shelter, health, education and yet are still bitter, afraid, and are not the "complete" human beings they could be. Christians see God as making possible that vital quality of "humanness"—a loving and fulfilling relationship to other persons and to the world—because of their belief that God cares for them personally and for the world which he created. Jesus is understood to be the key person in the relationship between God and humankind. God has made Jesus the bridge between himself and those who believe in him and between each person and his or her neighbor. Peter, one of Jesus' twelve disciples, declares the conviction of most Christians: " 'God has made this Jesus whom you crucified both Lord and Christ.' " (Acts 2:36 JB) What it means for a Christian to believe and live as if Jesus is "Lord," and thus "master" or "savior," of this fuller life will be studied further as we look at the stories of faith in this book.

This Christian belief or faith in Jesus Christ, held by millions of persons, has clearly affected the course of human history. The Christian faith has been an inspiration for both peace and war. It has motivated causes which benefited humanity and acts of cruelty which shamed humanity; it has influenced revolutions and reformations; and it has inspired countless works of art and music over the centuries. As our Western civilization has grown, it is difficult to think of an area of human activity that has not felt the effect in some way of the Christian religion. Even those who would not consider themselves Christian or even religious, in the popular sense of the word, have had the ordinary, everyday events of their lives influenced by Christians. Some of the values held by these Christians become part of our own story, our history, and the Western culture.

Diversity of Christian Beliefs

The Christian tradition influences everything from the motto of the United States stamped on its coins, "IN GOD WE TRUST," and the use of the Bible in courts of law, to the words of popular songs like, "Amazing Grace" and "Morning Has Broken." However, Christians often have difficulty understanding or explaining to others what their belief means. Sharing the meaning and importance of what Christians believe becomes even more difficult when this worldwide religion is divided into at least three main groups with different viewpoints:

ROMAN CATHOLIC   EASTERN ORTHODOX
PROTESTANT

The latter of these, Protestant, contains some 250 different subgroups called denominations. There are also many Christians, including Baptists, Christian Scientists, Mormans, and Pentecostals who do not consider themselves to fit into any of these groups, yet they are also an important part of the Christian community. Each of these branches of the Christian church has a distinctive emphasis, a unique history, and characteristic beliefs and practices. With all this richness and diversity, it is sometimes hard even for Christians to know which "Christianity" one is talking about. The difficulty of understanding and explaining may be reduced if we can develop a mental picture of the trunk of this massive tree of Christianity. By tracing the roots of Christianity's setting and historical development, by examining the fiber of its basic beliefs and practices, and by observing the flowering of its rituals and patterns of celebration, we may have a more comprehensive image of this world wide religion.

The purpose of this study is to assist the reader in learning about Christianity by viewing this religion as one would a weathered oak tree that has stood for generations, maturing to provide shelter and support to a variety of people, through succeeding ages, in all seasons. That same tree of Christianity has been nourished by the particular soil and climate in which it was planted and shaped by the factors that it encountered from the natural and human setting. It has survived lack of nourishment, being buffeted by storms and even the attempts of individuals or communities to lop off a limb or cut it down. However, that tree looks different in new seasons and it will be remembered differently as a sapling than as a mature plant. Therefore, many people will view Christianity from varying perspectives, seasons, and branches.

The Impact of Christianity

This introduction to Christianity attempts to expose you, whether it is your first look or whether you have been studying the tree for years, to the core of Christianity—its history, commitments, and rituals. The study seeks to be *descriptive* as it examines the trunk of this great tree of religious tradition. It tries to be *evaluative* in acknowledging the failures and tragedies of the Christian faith as well as its contributions and promises. It strives to be *experiential*—namely, rooted in shared experience so that it is clear that some of the values at the core of the Christian religion have become so widely accepted that they may affect our thoughts, feelings, and actions even if we do not believe that these values are true or persuasive. Further, it seeks to be *appreciative* of the millions of people through the centuries who have believed in and acted upon the Gospel, which means "good news," of the Christian message. These Christians have significantly affected the language, relationships, thought forms, and institutions of Western culture. Thus the aim of this study is to lead the reader to a basic understanding of Christianity, to help evaluate it critically, and to enable the reader to interpret Christianity for him or herself and others.

Religion as Relationship

One of the initial steps in understanding the Christian religion is to move back for a look at what religion means. There are many definitions of religion. Some emphasize the intellect or how a person thinks: "I believe God wants me to forgive the person who threatened my family." Other definitions stress the emotions or how we feel: "God makes me feel joyful or complete." Others identify areas of human behavior that are influenced by beliefs such as ethics, rituals, and personal experiences. Still other definitions of religion aim at one's connection to a special individual or organization: "I believe that Jesus cares about me personally" or "I am a member of the Christian church."

When archaeologists, anthropologists, historians, and other scientists examine human history, they indicate that virtually every tribe and community throughout recorded history has had some form of religion. Humankind has always worshiped, that is, responded with honor, devotion, or love to that which persons hold worthy of supreme value. In fact, the word religion comes from the Latin term *religio*, which means "to bind." Religion is concerned basically with relationships. One important function of religion is to establish a meaningful relationship between individuals or communities and that which they value. The person, reality, or value which one considers worthy of commitment is naturally something with which he or she seeks to establish a relationship. So the follower of a religious belief might say "God demands...," "My group expects...," or "My leader hopes...." Each statement suggests a response to a relationship.

Religion as Ultimate Concern

Paul Tillich, a famous twentieth century philosopher and religious scholar, is helpful in describing this idea of commitment when he says that religion, in the widest sense of the word, means ultimate concern. To be religious is to be grasped by an ultimate concern which qualifies or makes secondary every other concern and contains an answer to the meaning of life. For example, if there is a conflict in your life that demands a choice, you would be willing to sacrifice lesser concerns for the sake of this central value or ultimate concern. Something is only genuinely an ultimate concern if it concretely affects the way you live: how you think, act, and feel; the kind of decisions you make about your relationship to other persons—friends and enemies; your response to the natural world; the way you use your time; how you think about death and the goals of life.

Religion points to that which we ultimately value. What we value is then expressed in our relationships to the other persons with whom we come into contact. According to Tillich's definition of religion, which the authors find helpful, any person who has a relationship to an ultimate concern that affects all the areas of his or her life is religious. The ultimate concern could be God as a Christian understands him through Jesus of Nazareth, but it could also be money, or another person, success, or a political philosophy. However, the one question that must continually be asked is whether a particular concern is truly ultimate. The test of religious conviction from the view of this study is whether one has a relationship to an ultimate concern that justifies such loyalty and influences the whole of a person's life, and whether there are expressions of this relationship in everyday decisions and actions. Ask yourself what you trust or value. What is most important to you at this moment in your life? Could your friends identify your ultimate concern?

Christianity as a Lived Religion

The Christian religion could be explained as the ideas in which a Christian believes, such as those found in a "creed." Christianity might also be seen as a series of ceremonies performed in a special place of worship. However, the authors feel the core of Christianity can best be understood through the ways that a group of persons called Christians respond to God as their ultimate concern. These people have gathered in communities called churches. It is in their celebration of worship that their beliefs or convictions are shaped and reinforced. Christianity is a "lived religion" that seeks to make what Christians believe and celebrate come alive in the pattern of their daily lives and in the quality of their relationships to God and to other people.

If relationships and values which express one's personal faith are central to what it means to be religious, then the all-important question in understanding the ultimate concern of followers of a religion like Christianity is: With whom does the Christian seek a relationship? What is the quality of life that emerges from that relationship? Another way of stating the issue is: Whom does the Christian believe in? How does this change the Christian's life?

The answer to these questions is both terribly simple and extremely complex. The Christian is related to God as known in Jesus. The values which shape this relationship are faith, hope, and love. A man named Paul, seen by most Christians as the first great missionary and theologian of the Christian church, declares in describing the quality of the Christian life, "There are three things that last for ever: faith, hope, and love; but the greatest of them all is love." (1 Corinthians 13:13 NEB) The simplicity and clarity of this basic Christian confession has amazed and startled generations. But the real difficulty comes as a Christian tries to apply these values of faith, hope, and love to the ordinary as well as to the traumatic events of life: How can someone be faithful to God? Who really cares for one's neighbor? What does it mean to have hope that God's goodness will ultimately prevail? What responsibility do Christians have in their use of the world as God's creation? How can any one person or community be creatively loving to the many who are in need? One of the goals of this text is to help the reader understand what it means for a Christian to believe in Jesus' promise of abundant life and to live out the basic Christian values in relationship to God, to other persons, and to the world.

Understanding Through Case Studies

Many dramatic statements can be made about Christianity:

Christianity has made an enormous impact on Western history and culture.

Modern society demonstrates the worldwide presence and influence of the Christian churches.

One out of four of the world's people claims to be Christian.

None of these facts may be very significant in understanding the Christian religion unless we observe how this lived-faith can and does shape personal lives and decisions. This volume includes several case studies. The ways in which the values and beliefs of Christians influence their personal choices may best be explored by studying these cases. A case is an actual account of persons making important decisions. Each involves both a situation and a decision about which reasonable men and women could disagree.

A case study should not be confused with an example. No "answers" are provided, precisely because in many of the important decisions of life no clear right or wrong answer appears. However, a good case study is not merely a slice of life which describes the events at a certain period in a person's life. A case should demonstrate the necessity of a decision which makes a difference in an individual's life. Although several creative and responsible solutions to each problem are possible, some may be better than others. The decision which is most creative and responsible is often not clear cut or obvious. You might be asked to attempt to understand and identify with the persons in each case and to suggest what decisions they could make and the one which *you* would make. Remember that the appropriate or best decision will be one that is consistent with your own beliefs. Thus you must know and be able to explain what your own beliefs and values are, as well as understand the problems presented in these cases.

It is an intriguing experience to be involved with a case study. In many ways a case is like a mystery story in which you are asked to determine the facts based only on the information provided, discover the possible clues or important questions, and finally decide and defend your alternative. One aim of this method is to develop and test your ability to analyze the situation sensitively and to try out your talent in proposing imaginative and helpful solutions which you can defend and for which you are willing to be held responsible.

Eyeglasses of Faith

"Theology" is a word some Christians use to describe their talk about God. Theology could be seen as an orderly way of understanding human life in the world from the viewpoint of faith in God. For the Christian theology may function like a pair of eyeglasses. If one looks at the world through the glasses of Christian faith, then the relationship to other persons and objects looks different. The glasses the Christians use are made up of the "resources of faith." The resources through which the Christian looks at life are the church's sacred literature (the Bible) and the church's special story (tradition). However, if we take off our glasses and study them rather than looking through them at the life around us, we will not see very clearly, and if we are especially near-sighted, we may even stumble and fall. That would be like studying only the history, beliefs, and celebrations of Christianity apart from its effect on individuals and communities. This kind of study will not be much help in deciding and doing. The Christian tries on the eyeglasses of faith to see more clearly what the world looks like. "Getting even" with a person who has hurt us may appear fair and necessary without glasses and look selfish and narrow through the glasses of faith that tell the story of Jesus insisting we are to forgive one another continually.

Trying on this pair of glasses, that is, seeing these case studies through a Christian perspective, may add a new viewpoint in a heated discussion on a possible teenage abortion, the topic of the first case study. With the increasing number of unwanted pregnancies among teenagers, the problem this case presents is very real for many high school and college young people. The Christian viewpoint raises questions in addition to whether an abortion would be safe, how much it costs, whether parents or friends will find out about it, if it is legally justified, and how the persons involved will feel about their decision.

The glasses of faith also ask: Is abortion the murder of a person created by God and intended as a "gift" to the world? Will an unwanted child limit the possibility of a full or abundant life for both the parents and the child? In light of the world's alarming birth rate, is the termination of potential life a responsible use of the freedom God has given us in relation to the world? The meaning and depth of the reader's ultimate concern may be called for in making these decisions.

The second case stretches your imagination to investigate the meaning of "love and "hope," key Christian values. How do these values influence a choice of whether a young couple should do voluntary service through the Peace Corps in South America or take a job at home in a parent operated company to gain skill and experience for later service? The third case is on freedom as seen through the eyes of a high school freshman struggling with her parents over hours, use of alcohol, and selection of friends. How can someone who is restricted by rules and regulations grow and mature? Who has the right to set these boundaries? The fourth case asks: what does the decision of a young girl to voluntarily choose an earlier death so a child can have access to life-saving medical equipment say about life after death for both adults and young people? By "trying on the eyeglasses" of faith and discussing the cases with the provided teaching and learning guide, the study of Christianity may become as exciting and challenging as was first intended.

Christianity is seen in this text as an important resource for making and understanding the decisions that face us in life. The sections that follow each of the four cases will provide important suggestions about several ways a Christian might see the problem and make a decision using Christian faith in God. The authors personally believe that the Christian faith offers a meaningful way of living fully and understanding life more clearly. However, even if the reader rejects a view of life influenced by a Christian perspective, the study of Christianity can be provocative and stimulating. The Christian view of the meaning of life has been persuasive to millions of persons. It commands serious consideration and respect by all as concerned citizens of a worldwide community in the same way that viewpoints reflected in other great religions of the world merit respect.

From the Christian Perspective

Some Christians see faith basically as a response to God or to the traditions of the church. Other Christians begin from a specific situation and see a fundamental guideline for a Christian's response in Jesus' words when he was asked which of God's commandments was most important. He replied: " ' "Love the Lord your God with all your heart, with all your soul, with all your mind." That is the greatest commandment. It comes first. The second is like it: "Love your neighbour as yourself." ' " (Matthew 22:37–39 NEB) Most Christians would interpret Jesus' words to mean that love is the standard by which a person's relationship to God and to other persons is judged. The Christian believes this is a special kind of love which is a gift from God.

Christianity, like all other religions has special words or terms that its followers come to understand and use. Several of these terms will be introduced now and filled out later. In addition to love, two other important elements of Christianity are illustrated when Jesus says, " 'I am the bread of life' " and " 'everyone who believes may have eternal life.' " (John 6:35, 3:15 JB) The Christian views both abundant life and eternal life as the result of a relationship to God as seen in Jesus. The promise of the Christian gospel is that one may become more complete and fulfilled because of this relationship to God. Christians believe that in Jesus they see a person who is really free, who has an ability to love others without hesitation, who knows who he is and can live in peace with himself and others. For Christians this is an illustration of what it means to be fully human or have abundant life. Jesus has been described as "the man for others." A relationship to Jesus, Christians believe, helps them become fulfilled as persons whose basic stance in life is to be "for others." The meaning of abundant life and eternal life will be explored in more detail later, particularly as they apply to the cases of human conflict described above.

Christianity has a crucial individual dimension. Christians are convinced of God's love for them. A person's response to this love then requires and allows him or her to make certain commitments of love and concern to others. However, Christianity is also a communal religion; it is the faith of a community of believers. Faith in God has been explained historically by members of communities from Moses and the prophets, so significant to the Jewish tradition, to Jesus and his disciples. This faith continues to be interpreted through the eyes of believers who are members of communities today. The way Christianity is linked to Judaism through belief in the same God is considered in the first section of this book, Setting and History.

A Preview

This study of Christianity is divided into three parts. Each section will include several major ideas or themes of the Christian faith:

Part I: Setting and Historical Development of Christianity

Part II: Basic Beliefs and Practices

Part III: Patterns of Celebration.

Each part employs one or two case studies to introduce the following two chapters. As you discuss the cases, try to apply what you have learned about Christianity to a concrete situation. To make the study more exciting, particularly for those discussing it in a group or course, and to allow each person to apply their learnings, there is a special "Resource Guide" on teaching and learning through cases. It contains suggestions on how to use each case, projects to enrich the discussion, films to illustrate the ideas, and additional projects and suggested readings. The Resource Guides to Chapters 2, 4, and 6 also contain suggestions of specific additional case studies which could be useful in highlighting central chapter themes.

The important themes of the Christian faith which intertwine and overlap each of these parts like the branches of a tree are as follows:

Central Christian values: Faith, Love, Hope.

Basic Christian convictions: God's Good Creation, Love of God and Neighbor, Eternal Life.

The issue is, will a consideration of these themes affect how one decides and acts? The challenge to understand these themes begins with "A Matter of Life or Death," the case of Sue Ann and the question of abortion. What would you say and do if you were Sue Ann or one of her close friends? This is an issue of the fullness of life. The problem is, for whom?

PART
I

Setting and
Historical Development

A MATTER OF LIFE OR DEATH
Case Study A

The antiseptic smell of a hospital had always made Sue Ann Thomas feel sick to her stomach. As she waited alone in the cold reception room, her mind flashed back to two weeks ago when she had first told Danny she was pregnant. He wasn't so much angry as he was confused and kind of dazed. They talked about what she could do. Sue Ann was sixteen, a junior at Central High, and she was afraid to tell her parents about the baby. Danny had finished high school last year and had a pretty good job in a garage in south Chicago. Together they could get up the $175 for an abortion.

Sue Ann remembered the name of Dr. Engles. Her mother had gone to him a couple of times. Making an appointment under another name, Sue Ann told him she was eighteen and that she wanted an abortion. Dr. Engles had talked to her after the pregnancy tests proved positive. He told her about a hospital in Chicago which had the best clinic for pregnancy termination he knew. While Sue Ann was still there, he called the hospital for a date, wrote out the papers for her to take in, and asked her to make an appointment with the nurse to see him three weeks after the abortion to make sure everything was all right. As Sue Ann walked out of the office, she thought that Wednesday—one week away—would never come soon enough.

The next week of waiting had been hell. Sue Ann was only six weeks along, but she was sure she would begin to show. When Wednesday came, Sue Ann told her mother she was going over to a girlfriend's house for supper so she would be home late. When Danny came by early that morning in his old Ford to take her to school on his way to work, Sue Ann was sure her parents would never know. Both her mother and her father had been bugging her for a couple of weeks now.

Her mother said she didn't look well and Sue Ann knew they were worried about her.

Danny and Sue Ann didn't say much on their way into the city. Danny was already going to be late for work so he let her out on the corner and said he'd pick her up after he got off work about 5:30. She had seemed so confident, so sure of herself last week—even this morning —but as she handed the papers to the receptionist and then paid the hospital cashier, she was aware of how cold and clammy her hands felt. She jumped when the nurse called her into a small office to take her blood pressure and temperature.

Dr. Engles had told Sue Ann what would happen during the day. There were five women in the large room with her—no one younger, and a couple of them seemed in their fifties. Sue Ann knew that at some time during the day before the "pregnancy termination" there would be a group counseling session with a social worker. She remembered a couple of weeks ago telling her closest friend, Sharon, that she was pregnant. Sharon had blurted out that she could never have an abortion—she would feel too guilty. Sue Ann realized that Danny was the only other person she had told about the baby. She was already afraid of having to talk with these women about it. Sue Ann chose a corner bed in the large ward room and stared out the window as she waited. It had begun to snow.

For the first time Sue Ann let herself think about Paul Reynolds. She hadn't dated anyone else during her first two years of high school. Paul was older, he went into the army, and they wrote to each other all last year. They planned to be married as soon as Sue Ann finished high school. But last summer the army found that Paul had a heart defect. He came home on an extended leave, then he died in July. Sue Ann still couldn't really believe it. She started dating Danny just before school began in the fall and they started going together in October. He was good company but nothing like Paul. She and Danny had a good time together, and he helped her forget. Paul had been a Roman Catholic. She remembered reading that the Catholic Church thought an abortion was just like murder. Sue Ann didn't want to think about what Paul would have said about the baby.

Getting an abortion had seemed like the only thing to do. It was all so easy. Sue Ann began to tremble. She wondered if the baby was a boy or a girl.

The social worker came in and introduced herself. The women began to talk, to tell their ages and their reasons for choosing to have an abortion. A girl in her twenties, who introduced herself as Mary, laughed uneasily and asked if anyone had ever backed out this far along. Connie Davies, the social worker, responded very seriously. "Yes, over the past six months of this particular program there have been three women who chose at the last minute not to terminate their pregnancies. That's one of the reasons I'm here to talk with you—to make sure you are clear about what you are doing."

Sue Ann dug her fingers into the bed sheets and began to feel the tears well up in her eyes. She had come this far. What could she do if she backed out? Sue Ann was the only one who had not spoken. Connie Davies turned to her and waited.

CHAPTER 1

God's Creation and Covenant

Both the Jewish and the Christian Bible begin with the same declaration:

> In the beginning God created the heavens and the earth.... God created man in the image of himself... male and female he created them.... God saw all he had made, and indeed it was very good. (Genesis 1 JB)

Christians as well as Jews affirm God as Father and Creator, sustainer and preserver of life. This Creator God, whom believers address as a loving parent, has also made a covenant, or a binding agreement with his children, that he will not abandon them but will continually be related to them in love. Both Christians and Jews believe that God, as both Creator and Father, is compassionately concerned about all his creatures and expects in response their love and loyalty. The Bible witnesses to a people's experience of faith and hope in a powerful, just, and merciful God.

The historical community of Israel, which dates back thousands of years, believed that human life is essentially good. This is also a basis of modern Jewish faith. All persons have dignity, worth, and responsibility not simply because they are born but because they are made in the image of God. As all persons have a special relationship to God as his creatures, they are called the children of God. This belief in God's creation and covenant or contract relationship is also a conviction shared by the Christian community.

The historical setting of Christianity does not begin with Jesus of Nazareth and his twelve disciples or with the Apostle Paul and his missionary journeys; it begins with a small nomadic group of people of

Semitic origin. Through a religious vision and the leadership of men like Moses, this people came to be known as the Israelite nation. They believed they were God's chosen people, destined to bring " 'a light to nations, that [God's] salvation may reach to the end of the earth.' " (Isaiah 49:6 RSV) Today's Jewish people, who share the great living religion of Judaism, are the descendants of these Israelites.

Earliest Roots of Christianity

Christianity is indebted to and forever linked with Judaism. Jesus himself was not a Christian but a Jew living in Palestine during the first century A.D. Jesus' teachings were based on much of the experience and faith of his people. Most statements by and about Jesus can best be understood in light of the promise and prophecy of the sacred literature of the Jews, which Christians describe as the Old Testament, the first part of their Bible.

Some people see Christianity as the fulfillment of Judaism. Jesus is understood by most Christians to be the Messiah foretold in the Old Testament. The name *Messiah* is often translated in the New Testament, the second part of the Bible, as "Christ." Thus the word *Christ* is not Jesus' last name but a title which literally means "anointed one." Some Christian scholars seek to illustrate this by calling him "Jesus, the Christ."

Whether or not one agrees with those Christians who believe that Jesus is the Messiah predicted in the sacred Jewish literature, an idea Judaism rejects, or that he is the divine Son of God sent to bring light and life to all persons, it is clear that Jesus did not see himself as contradicting the basic faith of the community of Israel. Jesus declares, " 'Think not that I have come to abolish the law and the prophets; I have come not to abolish them but to fulfil them.' " (Matthew 5:17 RSV)

The setting for Christianity is in the story of the people of Israel and in the relationship of these people to God as Creator and Father. However, this story, as recorded in the Jewish sacred literature, was not intended to be a scientific history or a simple description of the events and activities of a particular people at a given period of time. It was meant to be a story of faith, a story of how the people were affected by their belief in God. These sacred writings which Christians came to call the Old Testament not only record the acts and encounters of Israel, they also record an interpretation of these events. God is believed to be working out his will in human history as he constantly involves himself in the lives of his people. Christians and Jews see God's creative and dynamic activity, God's "self-disclosures," as the decisive factor in Israel's history.

The various stories of the Bible were written from the commitment and belief or faith of one particular community and addressed to the faith of another community that could understand and hear it correctly. In the same way, the Christian hears and sees this story of Israel not only through the eyes of belief in God the Father and Creator but also through faith in this same God who is most clearly revealed and understood in Jesus, the Christ. Christians see the account in the Old Testament from a particular angle, or with an added dimension. They understand this account of one community's encounter and interaction with God to be a preparation for God's ultimate self-disclosure of himself and his purpose for the world through Jesus Christ. A Christian view of history puts Jesus at the center with historical events leading up to and from his birth. The modern calendar follows this concept in its use of B.C. and A.D., abbreviations for "before Christ" and *Anno Domini*, meaning "in the year of the Lord" or when Christ was born.

The Bible: Its Development

The Christian religion, because of its historical understanding of the Jewish tradition and the coming of the Christ, divides its sacred literature, the Bible, into two major sections: the Old Testament (or Covenant) which is the same as the Jewish Bible, and the New Testament. The word Bible literally means "book," and the Christian Bible contains from sixty-six to seventy-three (depending on the version of the Bible used) separate books. These books include examples of myth, legend, history, philosophy, prophecy, and law. In these books is a variety of literary types, from poetry and drama to the short story and informal letters. Some Christians consider the Bible to be the directly inspired word of God and thus to be taken as literally true. Other Christians, while denying the Bible is or was intended to be literally true, consider it to be a reliable witness of God's word to all persons. However, all Christians would affirm that the Bible is a guide to Christian faith and conduct. Christians agree that the great moments of God's revelation, or his communication of himself to men and women, are recorded and interpreted in these writings.

The complete Bible as it is known today was a long time being written, nearly one thousand years. It was almost two thousand years ago, only after much testing and argument, that the canon, or standard list of books to be included in the Bible, was finally established. The Jewish scriptures which Christians call Old Testament canon were determined by a council of rabbis at the end of the first century A.D. There were about a dozen books, called Apocrypha, which were not contained in the approved list of Jewish scriptures. Therefore, in different versions of the Bible the Apocrypha may be included in the Old Testament, printed in a separate section, or omitted altogether. The accepted list of books to be included in the New Testament was finally established by the end of the fourth century A.D.

This ancient and diverse group of writings has been translated into over one thousand languages and has had more copies distributed and sold than any other book in the history of the world. "Why," one might ask, "are the writings in this book, which has provoked so much controversy and conversation through the years, so important to Christians in the twentieth century?" Is it because the Bible has been so widely distributed that it has been described as "the foundation of Western culture?" Or is it because the characters, events, images, and language of the scriptures have so penetrated everyday experience that a person cannot read the daily newspaper, listen to folk or popular music, see street posters or museum murals without encountering things which test or draw upon one's knowledge of the Bible? References to the Garden of Eden, Noah's Ark, the Ten Commandments, Judas' "thirty pieces of silver" earned for betraying Jesus, the Nativity scene at Christmas, and the cross of Jesus all depend on the knowledge of people and events described in the Bible. For most Christians, however, these facts about the influence of biblical literature do not provide a sufficient answer to why this book is relevant today.

The teacher of a high school English class studying the modern novel came in one morning and asked his class which book was the all-time bestseller. After a few wild guesses one student shouted, "I know: the Bible." The teacher agreed with the answer, took a copy of the Bible from his desk, and tossed the book to the floor. The surprised class asked, "Why did you do that?" "The importance of the Bible is not dependent on how it looks, how it sells, or even on how it is revered in religious circles. The importance is in the power of the stories it contains and in their effect on the reader."

The Bible as a resource and a guide has power and importance as it "comes alive" for the reader. This collection of books is important if it makes contact with human experience and informs, enlightens, contradicts, or troubles people's thoughts and actions. Many Christians consider this crucial, because they believe the Bible continues to reveal God's purpose for life.

The Bible: A Modern Resource

The Bible has been described as both a record of God's search for man and of man's search for God. The truth probably lies in between—in the numerous *encounters* between God and his people. The Bible contains testimony of God's initiative in relation to others. God chooses. God promises. God demands. God claims and receives obedience, trust, and love. Abraham, the father or first patriarch of the nation Israel encountered God who declared,

> "Go from your country and your kindred and your father's house to the land that I will show you. And I will make of you a great nation, and I will bless you ... and by you all the families of the earth will bless themselves." (Genesis 12:1–3 RSV)

God called on Abraham to leave the security of his father's land, to take his own family and possessions and go to a strange land. The demand was to trust his life to God. God took the initiative and made a covenant with Abraham to bless and care for him and his descendants. Abraham's response to this encounter was astounding, given the circumstances. "So Abram [Abraham] went, as the LORD had told him." (Genesis 12:4 RSV) This response of faith and obedience to an encounter with God made possible the fulfillment of God's call and purpose.

There are also biblical encounters between God and humankind characterized by unfaith, judgment, and forgiveness. King David ordered one of his soldiers killed and then took that man's wife, Bathsheba, for his own. The prophet Nathan learned of this, went to David, and told him the story of a rich man who had many sheep. According to the story, a visitor came and the rich man took the only thing a poor neighbor possessed, a little ewe lamb, and had it prepared for the guest's dinner. When David heard the story, he was angry with the rich man and said, " 'The man who has done this deserves to die.' " Nathan said to David, " 'You are the man.' " Later, when David confessed and repented, God said, " '[I have] put away your sin; you shall not die.' " (2 Samuel 11, 12 RSV)

In the New Testament a woman was saved by Jesus as she was about to be stoned by a crowd for being caught in the act of adultery. Jesus quietly spoke to the people, " 'Let him who is without sin among you be the first to throw a stone at her.' " One by one the people turned and slipped away until Jesus was alone with the woman. He looked at her and said, " 'Neither do I condemn you; go, and do not sin again.' " (John 8:1–11 RSV) Unfaithful encounters with God reap judgment and the brokenness of the relationship. But confession is followed by God's forgiveness and renewal of the relatedness.

The encounter between God and humankind may also be healing and restoring, which are themes of the dramatic account of Jesus raising Lazarus from the dead. In this story Martha and Mary were mourning for their dead brother, Lazarus. Their sorrow was even greater because Jesus had not come to them in time to heal Lazarus before he died. When Jesus did arrive, he responded to the sisters with words which are held to be a promise to all Christians: " 'I am the resurrection and the life; he who believes in me, though he die, yet shall he live, and whoever lives and believes in me shall never die.' " Jesus then went to the tomb, commanding Lazarus to come out. "The dead man came out, his hands and feet bound with bandages, and his face wrapped with a cloth. Jesus said to them, 'Unbind him, and let him go.' " (John 11:1–44 RSV)

These strange and often exciting stories have one theme that weaves through a thousand distinct accounts and sayings: human existence is a matter of life and death. Life is full when one is related to God by faith; there is death if that relationship is broken by unfaith. God created life and has made a covenant, or agreement, with those who encounter him in faith. Christians believe that God made a new covenant through Jesus Christ and that those who are related to God through Christ will reap the fullness of life: freedom, love, and peace. For Christians the biblical stories are significant because they may become personal stories.

A young man awakened in the early morning in a city apartment to the smell of smoke and the crackle of fire. He raced from the flaming apartment in sheer panic and ran through thick smoke down six flights of stairs. Not until he was in fresh air on the street below did it dawn on him that in his panic to save his own life, he had left his family still asleep in the apartment. The stairwell, now blocked by flames, sentenced them to death in their own beds.

Although the young man lived that night, he died inside. "I felt condemned by myself, my family (if they ever knew), and God," he confessed. Months later he heard the story of Lazarus (John 11) in the unlikely setting of a political discussion on party renewal. The young man saw himself bound up by his own guilt, as Lazarus was wrapped in the burial cloths. Breaking through the context of a political rally, Jesus' promise for new life and hope reached across the pages and the centuries, grasped and transformed this young man. Jesus' story became his ultimate concern, his story, his promise, part of his experience. "I felt as if the story was read not as a political parody, but for me, personally. I felt as if I had been freed from a kind of living death." Here the power of the biblical message of life broke through the centuries, the situation, and the language and came alive. It became a story from faith to faith.

Christians see the content of the Bible as one resource for understanding life and the world. It is a written history of how communities and individuals have given voice and form to what they value. It is a history of hope and despair, of failure and success, but always of encounter and relationship, of betrayal and renewal. Christians believe that the breaking and renewing of the Old Testament covenant between God and humankind comes to a dramatic climax in Jesus Christ,

in his death and resurrection, and in a renewed covenant which re-
establishes the relationship between God and his people. However, we
must not get ahead of the story, but rather return to the creation stories
of Genesis and the beginning of God's encounter with his people as
seen through the Christian perspective of faith.

The Old Testament Through a Christian Perspective

1. A Good Creation

It is appropriate that a brief account of the setting and historical
development of the people of God begins where the principal resource
of Christianity, the Bible, begins—with creation. The creation story was
put in the form of a poem, for poetry has the power to tell concisely and
beautifully, with comprehensive images, what both Christians and
Jews believe: every person is a creature or child of God the Father
and is made in his image. The decision of Sue Ann and Danny about
abortion cannot be seen simply as a practical or utilitarian question—
at least not from a Christian perspective. Christians link the creative
process to God and thus affirm it as "good." Any decision Sue Ann and
Danny make has serious implications for how one understands life as
"a gift of God."

There are actually two stories of Creation in Genesis. The first,
quoted at the beginning of this chapter (Genesis 1:1–2:4a), describes
"God" as "creating" the heavens and the earth, day and night, land
and water, vegetation and animals, man and woman, by the power of
his divine word in six days. The second story (Genesis 2:4b–3:24)
probably earlier in origin, focuses on the "LORD God" who "forms"
man (Adam), takes from his rib woman (Eve), and places them in the
Garden of Eden with tasks and responsibilities to both their creator and
their world.

Modern biblical scholarship indicates that the first story probably
did not come to its final poetic form until the sixth century B.C., nearly
seven hundred years after the Exodus when Moses led the Israelites out
of slavery in Egypt. However, neither the two separate accounts nor
the later date of writing need confuse the reader. The aim of the stories,
scholars declare, is not primarily concerned with saying scientifically
or descriptively how humankind came to be, but to define what hu-

manity *is* and, through the eyes of creation faith, what human existence *means*.

Both stories are needed, each in its own poetic and symbolic way, to give adequate expression to the faith of Israel that the true nature of a person, to be fully human, is to experience life in a relationship with God. Christians and Jews believe God is responsible for the creation of the world, through whatever process or span of time. Some Christians believe it was in six days through God's direct act; other Christians believe God creates through the natural evolutionary development of the world. However, most Christians agree that this creation, including human life, is *essentially good*. God pronounced it, from the beginning, "very good." For this reason the quality of human life is valued as precious and even sacred. This is true for the Christian and the Jew because both believe that life in all its fullness is a gift of God for which they are held responsible.

This account in Genesis affirms not only that life is good, but also that people, as the primary objects of God's love, become responsible before God for how they live life and how they respond to fellow creatures and care for the world placed under their dominion and care. Thus if Sue Ann and Danny deal with the question of abortion from a Christian perspective, one of their considerations might be of the fetus as a "potential person" who is a gift of God and one given into their care.

2. Freedom and Responsibility

The Christian understands that in "loving creation" God gave the human race tremendous freedom; humankind is almost a partner in creation. However, this freedom requires persons to understand and choose between alternative ways of valuing and acting. The story of Adam and Eve in the Garden of Eden portrays the beginning of human freedom and the responsibility for one's decisions. Encouraged by the serpent, Eve and then Adam break God's command by eating the forbidden fruit (Genesis 3). The notion of evil in the form of a serpent and sin represented by the human desire and choice to eat fruit from the forbidden tree symbolically illustrate the problem of human existence. How do the decisions of life affirm both one's freedom *and* responsibility? To be fully human means to maintain a relationship to the Creator that includes responsible obedience. To be fully human also means to exercise this freedom creatively when choices may result in a different style and quality of life.

What the Christian community values and hopes to communicate by retelling Israel's story of creation as its own is not merely the story of birth but the hope of a quality of life containing richness and potential for relationship to God and one's neighbor's. The faith of Israel emphasizes that each person has been given the gift of life by the love of God the Father and is responsible for the quality of that life. Both Sue Ann and Danny, in our case study, have a responsibility to one another as well as to their parents and their unborn child. Perhaps it might not be responsible or loving for Sue Ann to bring a child into a home situation where the baby is only tolerated and not really desired or loved. Another consideration for many Christians would be the extent to which Sue Ann would threaten her own fullness of life and Danny's if she leaves school now and, at sixteen, assumes the responsibility for family life. Each person is responsible for what he or she values. These values are reflected in people's thoughts, feelings, and actions.

3. Making a Covenant

What the Christian community values is shaped by its history and by those contracts or agreements which determine one's relationship to God and one's neighbors. The Christian story is not only about faith in God but about covenant faith in God. *Covenant* is an extremely important biblical word. Not only is it difficult to translate adequately from the Hebrew language, in which the Old Testament was written, but biblical scholarship also indicates that there are several ideas of covenant even in the Old Testament. It is clear, however, that covenant points to a relationship between God and humankind that is similar to a contract, treaty, or agreement. The initiative for the agreement is with God. He makes and binds himself to Israel. God makes unconditional promises for the future. Then the party to the covenant, such as Abraham, is obligated only to trust and obey. This is much more than a simple one-way agreement between a king and a slave, because persons are free to respond or not to respond to the initiative of God. If humankind responds to God, then the parties to the covenant come to have a relationship of mutual love and responsibility. They are not equal partners, but mutually binding obligations emerge. Israel completed a two-way covenant at Sinai following the Exodus and liberation from Egypt when the people promised to love and obey God. Israel believed that God demonstrated his covenant promise in creating the nation.

The biblical covenant and its renewal are usually sealed by a sign or reminder of the agreement. After the great flood in which only Noah and his family were saved, God sealed the covenant with Noah by a rainbow (Genesis 9:8–17). Abraham circumcised his children as a sign of his covenant with God (Genesis 17:9–14). Jews throughout the world still continue the practice of circumcision as a symbol of this promise. Jacob's name was changed to Israel when God promised that " 'a nation and a company of nations shall come from you.' " (Genesis 35:11 RSV) Jacob sealed the covenant by setting up a pillar of stone (Genesis 35:14–15). A covenant—like a pact between two friends, parties, or countries—asserts, "I have confidence that you will be loyal to our agreement and maintain our relationship with responsibility." The biblical story is founded on the covenant that God makes and keeps with people.

The recorded history of Israel began with the making of a covenant, cited earlier, between God and Abraham, who came to be regarded as the father of the nation Israel. He was a man seen by Jews, Christians, and even Moslems as the "friend of God." Historical and archaeological research reinforces to some degree the account that Abraham led a Semitic tribe of people from Ur in Mesopotamia perhaps about 1800 B.C., to settle in the land of Canaan, "the promised land" or "the holy land." This was later called Palestine and was located mostly in the present state of Israel and the kingdom of Jordan.

The meaning or significance of this story for Christians is that through Abraham, God chose his people, Israel, to be a servant and a witness of the Lord God "to all nations." God chose Israel neither because it was a large tribe, nor a small tribe, but because he loved it. The faith of Israel confesses that God, through the covenant he made with Abraham, promised to be their God and to care for and bless them through all generations. Israel learned, and the New Israel (the Christian church) affirmed, that this role of servant would be that of a suffering servant. It was a covenant not of privilege but of responsibility to be faithful to God and share his word and love with all peoples.

4. Breaking the Covenant

The biblical stories are not only of faith but also of lack of faith. Abraham, the people of Israel, and members of the early church were to break the covenant many times by their lack of loyalty and trust in God as the creator and sustainer of life. However, God kept the covenant and is constantly forgiving his people and restoring or renewing the covenant. In each renewal it becomes clearer what God values and expects in the relationship with his people. These renewals are evident in God's successive encounters with the other patriarchs, Isaac and Jacob, and with the twelve sons of Jacob and their families who took refuge in Egypt and then were enslaved. The biblical story then focuses on Moses, the father of Judaism and the earliest historic founder of one of the world's great living religions. Moses, through God's election and guidance, helped give birth to the historic nation of Israel in about 1250 B.C., by leading the Exodus. He participated in establishing a crucial renewal of the covenant at Mount Sinai (see Exodus 1–24).

5. The Exodus

The Exodus event becomes the great symbol which shapes the self-understanding of the community of Israel. This event explains in a dramatic and compact form what the community believes about life: God intervenes in human history. He discloses himself to Abraham, Moses, the prophets, and all who believe. Jews and Christians alike believe that God grasped the Israelites with an ultimate concern that compelled them to respond to him in love and service. They both believe that God delivered his people out of Egypt, out of human bondage. By confronting the powers of the world, represented in the Pharaoh, God granted his people freedom and dignity. This liberation and sense of worth was not due merely to the escape from Egypt, it was also due to a new relationship with God who shared himself with the people. The Israelites placed great significance on telling one's name to another. This was a sign of giving part of oneself and thus power to someone else. God gave himself symbolically to his people as their God when he shared his name with Moses (Exodus 3:14). *Yahweh* came from the Hebrew consonants *YHWH* (vowels in Hebrew of this time were not written out). It was in reverence and awe of God's power that the custom arose in later Judaism of not speaking the proper name of God. In reading *Yahweh* a person would substitute *Adonai,* which means "the Lord." An English translation of *Yahweh* is sometimes "Jehovah."

Both Jews and Christians affirm that God acted directly in history at the time of the Exodus and that he continues to intervene in human lives. It is God who is the author of the law; Moses was only the communicator who received the tablets of stone on which the famous Ten Commandments were recorded (Exodus 20). These instructions became a basis for Jewish and Christian ethics and have greatly influenced the legal structure and moral values of Western culture. The Commandments have authority first as God's law, not humanity's, and provide guidelines for a fulfilled relationship between humankind and God and between neighbor and neighbor.

To be fulfilled in the biblical sense means to be in a covenant relationship with God and therefore responsible to God and one's fellow creatures. The Exodus is understood by both Jews and Christians as showing humankind's liberation and dependence at the same time. It promises freedom for the fullness of life and freedom from oppressive forces within. However, it also means responsible and loving dependence on God as the Creator and the giver of life.

Sue Ann and Danny have been liberated, if one looks through the Christian glasses, to make their own decision about the fetus and the quality of their lives in the future. At the same time a responsible decision must take into account the interests of other persons with whom they have a dependent relationship. What burdens will fall on Sue Ann's parents if she bears the child? Or on society, not only in the form of taxation necessary for aid to dependent children, but the increasingly serious problem of world population that already threatens the existence and quality of life for all people on the earth? On the other hand, what responsibility does Sue Ann have to care for the fetus dependent on her? For a Christian, any decision about abortion has many implications for being responsible to other persons and to God. The Christian may not treat any life, present or potential, lightly. Life is more than mere existence; the *quality* of one's life is very important.

Creation and covenant illustrate one of the distinctive elements of Judaism and Christianity: God the Father is understood as a *personal* God who deals with his children through love and justice. Believers declare that God discloses himself in the midst of human history; he has made a covenant and guaranteed an inescapable relationship with his people. This is inescapable because God is constant. He is always judging each person in his or her loving faithfulness, and God is always forgiving each person's injustice, cruelty, and unfaith by renewing the covenant relationship. In response, all persons, as they are created in the image of God and capable of relationships, are expected to love and care for one another.

6. Kings Encounter the Covenant

In broad outline, the story of the Old Testament scriptures moves from the Judges, leaders in the early years of the nation, to the great Israelite kings of the tenth century B.C. such as Saul, David, and Solomon. David is remembered in the biblical tradition as the greatest king of Israel. He was the man of faith, the king who renewed the covenant with God. He was a musician, warrior, wise ruler; " 'the LORD is with him.' " (1 Samuel 16:18 RSV) He was also the man of unfaith who stole his soldier's wife and betrayed the covenant with God. Yet he returned to God to confess and renew the covenant. Solomon, whose wisdom is legendary, also carried out the construction of the first temple in Jerusalem. Later, in 587 B.C., the Babylonians invaded the kingdom of Judah destroying the cities, burning Solomon's temple, and carrying off the people of Israel to exile in Babylonia. This incident was understood by the Jews as God's judgment for the people's worship of Baal and other idols (acts of unfaith which violated the covenant). In 538 B.C. Cyrus of Persia conquered Babylonia and allowed the Jews to leave captivity and return to Palestine where they eventually rebuilt the temple in Jerusalem. Beginning in 322 B.C. the Jews were successively under Persian, Greek, Syrian, and Roman political domination until the destruction of the second temple in A.D. 70 and the final great dispersion of the Jews throughout the Roman Empire.

7. Prophets Interpret the Covenant

During this entire period of war and peace, a consistent theme echoed through one of the greatest collections of religious writing known to man: " 'Hear O Israel: The LORD our God is one LORD; and you shall love the LORD your God with all your heart, and with all your soul, and with all your might.' " (Deuteronomy 6:4-5 RSV) Divine promise and fulfillment is recorded from the Pentateuch (the first five books—Genesis, Exodus, Leviticus, Numbers, and Deuteronomy) to the historical books (Judges, Samuel, and Kings), from the "wisdom literature" of Job and Psalms to the major and minor prophets. The prophets were men who spoke to the Israelites as special messengers of God. Perhaps the prophets best represent this tradition of declaring and interpreting the covenant and creation faith of the people of God. Prophets such as Isaiah and Jeremiah altered the history of Israel and the faith of the community. The prophets' contribution was in interpreting the will of God in relation to the events of their time. They called for revolutionary reforms in social, political, and religious practice. Many people have referred to Martin Luther King as a twentieth century prophet. He was a man devoted to the fullness of life with love and justice and was convinced of the power of God. Yet he was murdered and his dream has not yet been fulfilled; the struggle continues. Future historians may declare that Martin Luther King altered the social history of the United States.

Prophecy persists as long as creation and covenant faith exist. The prophets believed they were called by God. They believed they spoke in the name of God, criticized the values that were contrary to God's will, and inevitably encountered hostility and opposition to their message. Their declarations have a contemporary ring of authenticity and truth.

For example, the prophet Jeremiah declared the judgment and demands of God: "Mend your ways and your doings, deal fairly with one another, do not oppress the alien, the orphan, and the widow, shed no innocent blood in this place.... You steal, you murder, you commit adultery and perjury ... you run after other gods whom you have not known; then you come and stand before me ... and say, 'We are safe.' ... I will not listen to you." (Jeremiah 7:5-10, 16 NEB) Yet hear also by Jeremiah God's promise to renew the covenant; " 'But this is the covenant which I will make with the house of Israel after those days, says the LORD: I will put my law within them, and I will write it upon their hearts; and I will be their God, and they shall be my people.' " (Jeremiah 31:33 RSV)

8. A New Covenant in the Messiah

The prophets continually called the people back to their covenant relationship with God. They also pointed out to the people signs of God's love for them. From the Christian perspective, passages in the book of Isaiah not only recall the covenant with God but also look forward to the fulfillment of the covenant promises in the coming of a Messiah, an "anointed one." This Messiah will be "a descendant of Jesse," from "the house of David." "There shall come forth a shoot from the stump of Jesse. . . . Righteousness shall be the girdle of his waist, and faithfulness, the girdle of his loins." (Isaiah 11:1, 5 RSV) The covenant purpose will be fulfilled in this Messiah: "They shall not hurt or destroy in all my holy mountain; for the earth shall be full of the knowledge of the LORD." (Isaiah 11:9 RSV)

Hope for the Messiah in the book of Isaiah reflects the pattern of a covenant or contractual relationship with God that needs renewing from time to time. The Messiah was seen as one who would renew this relationship. Christians understand the poetic imagery of the prophet Isaiah as descriptive of Jesus.

> For to us a child is born,
>   to us a son is given,
> and the government will be upon his shoulder,
>   and his name will be called
> "Wonderful Counselor, Mighty God,
>   Everlasting Father, Prince of Peace." (Isaiah 9:6 RSV)

In the religion of Judaism these questions were debated: who was the Messiah and when would he come? Was he an individual person or a remnant of Jewish people? When would he come to restore the covenant and thus renew the creation? Christians did not doubt who the prophet Isaiah was describing. Jesus of Nazareth came to be called the Messiah, the Christ, because, in light of Christian belief, the whole Old Testament pointed toward him as God's ultimate act for humankind.

Christians believe that Jesus came to restore the covenant relationship with God through his own person and thus to renew creation as the new or second Adam. The New Testament describes a new covenant that has connections with the original covenant. It was initiated by God and has mutual obligations. It is dependent on God's power and love. Yet Christians see it as a new and better covenant because it focuses on Jesus Christ, whom the Christian community believes can and does fulfill the covenant promises. Jesus the Messiah may secure the relationship between God and humankind that brings fullness of life because Jesus is both completely God and completely human. He becomes the link or mediator between God and humankind, between life and death.

The Christian faith came to understand Jesus as the center of the most important period in the history and development of Christianity. This period, described in Chapter 3, is recorded and interpreted, again from faith to faith, in the New Testament (New Covenant) understood by Christians to be a continuation (Hebrews 9:11–23) and the fulfillment (2 Corinthians 3) of the Old Testament (Old Covenant).

CHAPTER 2

Christ's Life and Love

From the Christian perspective the entire Old Testament faith in creation and covenant comes to a climax in the life and love of Jesus of Nazareth. By modern standards of biography, however, pitifully little is known about this obscure Jewish carpenter born in Palestine under the rule of Herod the Great in about 4 B.C. Even the reckoning of the Western calendar, which claims to be determined by the date of his birth, is almost certainly off a few years. Little or nothing is known about his physical appearance. Virtually the entire record of his life is contained in four brief essays called the Gospels and a small collection of letters and other writings that constitute the New Testament. However, many of these "books" were not even begun until thirty years after Jesus' death. Contemporary biblical scholars continue to debate about what Jesus actually said and did and what the earliest Christian community *believed* about his actions and words. However, as scholars now note, no serious secular historian today doubts that Jesus existed. The question is, what do the events of Jesus' birth, life, and death *mean?* How would they, or could they, affect the quality of one's life today?

The Gospels: Testimony and Transformation

The public life of this itinerant preacher was at most a few years. He was not the author of any books, and most scholars agree that many of his major teachings are found in a parallel form in literature of that period. Yet nearly two thousand years later, Jesus' birth and death are celebrated by millions across the world. The words of Jesus reported in the New Testament could all be spoken in about two hours. Yet his sayings, stories, and suggestions for life are quoted more often than those of any other figure in the history of humankind. Jesus has been described by people and nations as King, Lord, Savior, Healer, Son of God, Prince of Peace.

How can one conceivably account for the tremendous influence of this man when the major source for knowledge about his life are the few books of the New Testament? The authors are suggesting that this may have happened because the transformation of a person's existence, the discovery of one's very self, begins not with ideas but with experiences. A story in Chapter 1 describes a young man whose family had been killed in a fire; his entire life was changed by a new understanding of Jesus' words. It is possible that Sue Ann, in her present crisis, may be open to a new understanding of the meaning of life for herself and those around her. The *core* of who one is may be affected by either a dramatic event or a progression of everyday occurrences. One is not changed by simple verbal acceptance of universal principles or philosophical wisdom. Persons are changed by a realization of how these beliefs affect their attitudes and their concrete decisions.

The biblical material straightforwardly declares that it tells a story in order that others may believe and therefore have their lives changed (John 20:31). The Gospels (Matthew, Mark, Luke and John—the first four books of the New Testament) are not biography, but testimony. The word *gospel* means "good news."

The Gospels recount, in a variety of styles and forms characteristic of several authors, how men and women believed they had encountered God amidst the rhythm of daily occurrences. This encounter with Jesus Christ, and therefore with God himself, changed their lives as their ultimate concern became a loving relationship to God and neighbor. This type of commitment on the part of early Christians can provide an essential insight into understanding the testimonial nature of the first four books of the New Testament. The facts of Jesus' life were recorded by people who believed he was the promised Messiah. The primary concern of the writers was to share this "good news" with others.

Other Books Relate to the Gospels

The setting and historical development of Christianity is based on the biblical writings as a whole. However, it is the New Testament story and, more specifically, the account of what Christians believed Jesus Christ said and did that has shaped the values of the past and present Christian community. The life, death, and resurrection of Jesus form the central focus of the four Gospels. His life is responded to and continues to be interpreted by the remaining books of the New Testament. These include: the Acts of the Apostles, the fifth book of the New Testament, which is also the story of the early Christian community or church; the Epistles or Letters of Paul, the great missionary (e.g., Romans and Corinthians 1 and 2); the pastoral Epistles (e.g., Timothy and Titus), which provide guidelines for the Christian life; and those books written during times of trial or persecution of Chriatianity to give assurance and hope (e.g., Hebrews and Revelation).

Many Christian scholars now suggest that the earliest book of the New Testament, Paul's first letter to the Thessalonians, was written as early as A.D. 50 and that the remaining books were composed during the next fifty to a hundred years. Written in a "marketplace" dialect of Greek called *koine,* to be distinguished from classical Greek, the twenty-seven books of the New Testament became the special literature of the Christian community. Although writings of Christian theologians through the centuries have been important and influential, they have never come to hold the same importance or authority as the biblical literature, which was believed to be closely associated with the life and time of Jesus and his disciples.

The New Testament for Christians is like the key passage in a great book that they keep reading again and again to make sure they understand what the whole story is really about. Christians are not always sure that others' interpretations agree with theirs, but they are convinced that this is the key passage for understanding the whole story. The life and love of Jesus of Nazareth and the response of those who had faith in him as the Christ are the heart of the New Testament story for Christians. The New Testament, like the Old, is basically a story from faith to faith. The core of this account of faith is explored in the following pages.

Grasping the Quality of Jesus' Life

1. Overview

Most scholars believe that the authors of the Gospels are primarily interested in witnessing and not in reporting historical data about Jesus' life. From the earliest, Gospel of Mark (about A.D. 70), to the latest, Gospel of John (about A.D. 100), the authors were giving testimony concerning what they believed was the meaning of Jesus' life. They intended to proclaim and persuade others that God had made this Jesus of Nazareth their Lord and Christ.

Each of the four Gospels has its own unique flavor and style. As most scholars agree, the Gospels were based on many oral traditions about Jesus and probably on some other written sources. There are, however, certain undisputed facts about Jesus' life and ministry. Born in Palestine around 4 B.C., according to the corrected calendar, Jesus grew up in or around Nazareth and was raised according to the Jewish customs of his time. In a traditional ritual of cleansing he was baptized by John, a prophet who excited the country by proclaiming the immediate coming of the kingdom of God. About the age of thirty Jesus began a career of teaching and healing that drew large crowds; he was controversial among religious and political leaders. In his brief career Jesus met such hostility for his words and actions that he was crucified like a common criminal in Jerusalem.

A bare outline of historical data, however, does not communicate a life any more than a person who knows your name, birthplace, and occupation knows who you really are. To *know* a person is to encounter and develop a relationship which allows one person to trust another and to have confidence in the kind of person he or she is. To appreciate the rhythm of someone's life is to know not only what a person does, says, or values, but also the power and quality of that life. The task of the Gospels was to encounter, interpret, and evaluate the quality of Jesus' life, the significance of his death and resurrection, the power of his love. Only then could the authors dare to declare who this Jesus really is that they had come to believe in unconditionally and with whom they wished to risk their faith, love, and hope.

2. Jesus' Actions

One of the more obvious concerns of the Gospels is with what Jesus did. How did he spend his time and energy? What were his concerns? How did he affect others? The answers are spelled out in the rather simple but profoundly eloquent stories of Jesus' relationship to God and his neighbors. Jesus' actions are expressed in everyday events of casting nets, planting seeds, drawing water, breaking bread, holding children, and forgiving failures. Yet the New Testament writers imply that Jesus transformed the common into the unique by the way he lived and cared for those around him. Jesus is the one person who is fully human because he alone was able to keep the creation covenant. This was because, Christians believe, Jesus was faithful in his unstinting, unrelenting love of God and his concern for stranger and friend alike. As evidence of this love, he extended himself in healing assistance and forgiveness to others. Christians believe that Jesus was continually hopeful because he believed and responded to life as if God *does* make all things whole again.

3. Stories of Love

The Gospels tell the concrete stories in which this essential Christian witness is confirmed. Jesus spent his time and energy teaching and healing persons. He developed relationships with them not only in the synagogues and towns, but also beside the lake and in their homes. He welcomed a loving relationship with other persons, regardless of their profession or past; he was nicknamed the "friend of sinners" because he invested his time with the despised persons of his age.

Matthew, a Roman tax collector hated by the people because of his profession, became one of Jesus' twelve chosen followers called disciples (Matthew 10:3). A modern humorous paraphrase of an encounter with Jesus which changed the life of another tax collector concludes Frederick Buechner's delightful book, *Wishful Thinking: A Theological ABC* (N.Y.: Harper & Row, 1973), pp. 99–100:

ZACCHEUS

The fact that his name begins with a Z is only one reason why Zaccheus makes a good place to stop. He appears just once in the New Testament, and his story is brief (Luke 19:1–10). It is also one of the few places in the Gospels where we're given any visual detail. Maybe that is part of what makes it stand out.

We're told that Zaccheus was a runt, for one thing. That is why when Jesus was reported to be en route into Jericho and the crowds gathered to see what they could see, Zaccheus had to climb a tree to get a look himself. Luke says the tree he climbed was a sycamore tree.

We're also told that Zaccheus was a crook-a Jewish legman for the Roman IRS who, following the practice of the day, raked in as much more than the going tax as he could get and pocketed the difference. When people saw Zaccheus oiling down the street, they crossed to the other side.

The story goes like this. The sawed-off shyster is perched in the sycamore tree. Jesus opens his mouth to speak. All Jericho hugs itself in anticipation of hearing him give the man Holy Hell. *Woe unto you! Repent! Wise up!* is the least of what they expect. What Jesus says is, "Come down on the double. I'm staying at your house." The mob points out that the man he's talking to is a public disaster. Jesus' silence is deafening.

It is not reported how Zaccheus got out of the sycamore, but the chances are good that he fell out in pure astonishment. He said, "I'm giving everything back. In spades." Maybe he meant it. Jesus said, "Three cheers for the Irish!"

The unflagging lunacy of God. The unending seaminess of man. The meeting between them that is always a matter of life or death and usually both. The story of Zaccheus is the Gospel in sycamore. It is the best and oldest joke in the world

The New Testament also relates the story of a prostitute whose devotion led her to wash Jesus' feet with her tears and wipe them with her hair. She was forgiven by Jesus and restored because of her faith in him (Luke 7:36–50). The servant of a Roman commanding officer was restored to health; a leper was made clean; the mother-in-law of Jesus' disciple Peter was cured of fever (Matthew 8:1–15)—all because of the healing touch of Jesus. Nicodemus, a ruler and teacher of the Jews, found that despite his great learning a new insight allowed him to be born again of the Spirit, i.e., to become a different kind of person because of his new relationship to God. (John 3:1–21). A story about a Samaritan, a people hated by the Jews, was told by Jesus to answer the question, "Who is my neighbor?" Jesus' response has made the term *Good Samaritan* a universal symbol for charity and compassion for those in need (Luke 10:29–37).

Christians believe that Jesus' concern for the health and well being of those around him is representative of his concerns for men and women everywhere, of every race and condition. Yet his ultimate concern seems to have been God's overwhelming love for humankind and each individual's need to receive this love and the new life it promised. Jesus shared both God's life and love with his neighbors. The effect Jesus had on those whose lives he touched is described by the authors of the Gospels as transformed, renewed, healed, or "saved." A relationship with Jesus Christ may have been traumatic, but the Gospels wish to communicate that it was ultimately restoring and life-giving.

4. Jesus' Miracles

There were, according to some accounts, even more dramatic acts of Jesus which came to be described as miracles. These include the feeding of thousands of people with seven loaves of bread and a few fish (Matthew 15:29–39), Jesus walking on the water in order to reach his disciples in a boat and dispel their fear (Matthew 14:22–33), and the raising of Lazarus after he had been dead for four days (John 11).

Many of the same events in the Gospel accounts have several different versions. The miracles seem to be recorded by Matthew to show that Jesus was the true Messiah expected by the Jews—the Messiah who fulfilled the prophecy of the Old Testament. With the use of symbols John's Gospel portrays Jesus as the Word of God and the light for all people. Regardless of how one interprets the miracle stories, as literal occurrence or symbolic truth (and there are clear differences of opinion in the Christian community), it is agreed by most Christians that the miracle stories give testimony to Jesus' intention "to live for others" and to overcome all barriers of the human and natural world. Jesus reached out to persons in the miracle stories to bridge the great obstacles in the relationship between God and humankind: doubt, deprivation, and even death. Christians believe that these expressions of faith by the writers of the New Testament proclaim that absolutely nothing can separate them from the love of God precisely because of what has been done by Christ (Romans 8:38–39).

It appears that Jesus performed very few of the miracles in crowds. He refused to give them as a sign from God; rather he seemed to perform miracles to demonstrate the power of faith. The Gospel writers characterize Jesus' acts by his concern for the lives of his brothers and sisters, the children of God their Father.

5. Jesus' Words

Actions may speak louder than words, but words interpret, instruct, and guide values and commitments. Jesus' words and teachings were also preserved in the Gospels and have become some of the most familiar statements in the English language. Consider some of his commandments: "Love one another as I loved you (John 15:12 DB)"; " 'You shall love your neighbor as yourself' " (Matthew 19:19 RSV); or "Whatsoever ye would that men should do to you, do ye even so to them" (Matthew 7:12 KJV). His assurances have spoken to Christians for centuries: " 'You shall know the truth, and the truth will set you free' " (John 8:32 NEB) or " 'Come to me, all you who labour and are overburdened, and I will give you rest.' " (Matthew 11:28 JB) Many of his parables or stories are remembered simply by the title. The Prodigal Son brings to mind the story of a young man who took his inheritance and then lost all of his money by wild living. He returned home a dejected, starving man to be greeted by a joyful and forgiving father (Luke 15:11–24). The stories are enhanced by the use of striking imagery, such as the man seeking to remove a speck from his brother's eye while not noticing the log in his own (Matthew 7:3).

Jesus' recorded words are not respected because of their originality; many of his ideas are indebted to the Jewish scriptures. The parables are not loved merely for their beauty or simplicity. What Jesus said is judged to be noteworthy by the Christian community because his words are an authentic reflection of his life and love for others. The Gospels proclaim that Jesus not only spoke these words but lived them. Therefore, the values and insights to be discovered here, Christians believe, are the words of life for all those who, in faith, "hunger and thirst" after integrity and after the true self.

No scholar can briefly summarize Jesus' teachings because they were addressed to specific persons in specific situations. The teachings come alive for the individual hearer only by faith. But perhaps you can catch the flavor of Jesus' words as he began his public ministry by announcing that, " 'The kingdom of God is at hand; repent, and believe in the gospel.' " (Mark 1:15 RSV) This "kingdom of God" (or "kingdom of heaven" in the book of Matthew) did not refer to political control. The rule of God was to extend over all parts of life. The kingdom meant the community of those who sought to live out their expression of love for their Lord and neighbors. The kingdom would be the ultimate expression of God's overwhelming love and care for persons.

In the thirteenth chapter of Matthew, Jesus tells many parables to illustrate the meaning of the kingdom of God. The kingdom is compared to a buried treasure, the smallest seed which can grow into a great tree, or a pearl of great price. In Jesus' words, " 'What gain, then, is it for a man to have won the whole world and to have lost or ruined his very self?' " (Luke 9:25 JB) The underlying theme of Jesus' message is that God will continue to love all people but that he calls them to recognize the incredible value of that love and respond to it. Jesus' teachings show the spread and sudden power of the rule of God. Christians later came to believe that the promised kingdom of God was already quietly at hand—in the person of Jesus himself. Most Christians also look forward to a more dramatic and final demonstration of God's love and power at the end of human history. This time is called the eschaton.

The quality of life required in this kingdom or community is summarized by Jesus in the Sermon on the Mount (Matthew 5) in which he specifically addressed his disciples. In this sermon qualities of humility, mercy, and peacemaking are affirmed as central to God's rule. Participation in this community is very demanding since Jesus' commands go contrary to the normal expectations of most cultures: love your enemies; turn the other cheek in love when you are struck; forgive seven times seventy; seek not the wealth, honor, and security of this world, but be as carefree as the birds of the air and the lilies of the field; seek only the kingdom of God. These very difficult demands, however, go hand in hand with God's repeated promise of a relationship with a loving father who ultimately seeks the welfare of his children even when they are unfaithful. From the Christian perspective, whether Sue Ann decides to have the abortion, give the baby up for adoption, or keep the child, she has the assurance of God's continued love. Some choices may be less acceptable to God than others. But God's love for Sue Ann does not require that she make only correct decisions.

Jesus' Life Interpreted by the Disciples

The Gospels give testimony to what Jesus said and did to introduce God's rule by faith. The New Testament authors, however, also incorporate their evaluation of the life of Jesus directly into the story itself. Who was this Jesus of Nazareth who has touched every element of society with the gift of life and yields the response of love and faith? The disciple Peter responded to Jesus' question, "Who do you say I am?" with an answer that speaks not only for the authors of the Gospels but also for most Christians throughout the world over the twenty centuries since that initial encounter. Peter declared, " 'You are the Christ, the Son of the living God.' " (Matthew 16:16 RSV)

Jesus Christ is understood to have become fully human in terms of God's creation; he kept the covenant by unconditional love of God and neighbor. Christians came to believe that this Jesus was also fully God or the divine Son of God. This is a mystery Christians cannot explain. Through the eyes of faith, this is the story not just of a man, although he was certainly that. It is also a story of God the Son, who had such a transforming effect on the persons he encountered that they confessed he was their Lord and Savior. It is not altogether clear what Jesus meant when he referred to himself as the Son of Man, but it is certain what the Christian community came to believe about him. This is dramatically displayed in the account given in the Gospels of Jesus' birth, death, and, most important of all, his resurrection from the dead.

1. Birth

Accounts of Jesus' birth must be seen in terms of who the Christian community believed him to be. Matthew and Luke provide a moving story of Jesus' miraculous conception, through the direct influence of God as Spirit on Mary, apart from Jesus' human father, Joseph. The virgin birth that occurred in the humble setting of a stable in Bethlehem was attended by shepherds, kings, and angels to announce the fulfillment of the Old Testament prophecy: "Born is a son, 'Emmanuel' " which means "God with us." There is no account of the virgin birth in the other Gospels or Epistles. Many believers in the Christian community, however, hold to the account of Jesus' birth in Matthew and Luke; this includes members of the Roman Catholic and Eastern

Orthodox churches. Whether one takes the account of Jesus' nativity literally or symbolically, most Christians agree that this was a sign of incarnation, that is, of God taking on the life and form of the man Jesus. Christians believe God did this in order to make whole again, or save, those persons who believe in him, and ultimately all humanity. This was a fantastic notion that God should become incarnate in human form—that, in the words of the Gospel of John, "the Word [God] was made flesh, and dwelt among us . . . full of grace and truth." (John 1:14 KJV) Christianity affirms that Jesus Christ came to disclose or reveal God to humanity and to reconcile the broken relationship or covenant between them. The evidence for this belief was found not only in the manner of his birth but also in the manner of his death.

2. Death

Jesus' words and acts were controversial. Many people in the New Testament were shown to be touched by his love and responded with love. Others were moved by Jesus' judgment of the hypocrisy of the religious establishment in its disregard for the poor. He pronounced this judgment in the name of God, and some responded with anger, saying Jesus was a revolutionary. Some said he threatened the religious order by seeming to encourage the breaking of the Ten Commandments. For example, his disciples picked wheat on the Sabbath when no work was permitted; Jesus even healed on this holy day. Perhaps more significant and threatening to the Jewish religious leaders was his reinterpretation of the Jewish law; he rejected such notions as "an eye for an eye" and said, " 'If someone slaps you on the right cheek, turn and offer him your left.' " (Matthew 5:39 NEB)

Because Jesus claimed to forgive sins, he was finally brought to trial before a Jewish court in Jerusalem on a charge of blasphemy, or showing contempt for God. There were also political reasons for his trial. During his lifetime Israel was a conquered nation under Roman rule and Jesus' attitudes were seen by some as subversive. Jesus' declaration that God the Father was ruler, and the claim made by Jesus' followers that he was King of the Jews, led to a charge of high treason before the Roman official, Pilate. Jesus refused to answer the charges. While Pilate washed his hands of the afffair, Jesus was carried off to be crucified on a cross between two convicted thieves in a place known as Golgotha, "place of a skull." He was nailed to a cross and hung there until dead. Yet even in death Jesus asked God's forgiveness for the two thieves and for those who had crucified him. He extended his love to those around him until the final moment when he gave his spirit to God's care and died.

Jesus was betrayed and turned over to the authorities by Judas, one of his twelve disciples. Jesus was then executed as a convicted criminal. Yet Christians through the eyes of faith came to use "Christ crucified" as a title of honor and the cross as the central symbol for the Christian faith. What can this tragic and violent end of Jesus' life on the cross mean to the Christian community? The crucifixion has been given many meanings. It is understood as a sacrifice by God for humanity, a ransom for human sin, or the atonement (making God and humankind "at one") through Jesus' redeeming act of love. No church has adopted officially a *single* understanding of the crucifixion, but most Christians agree that Jesus' death on the cross is central to understanding Christian faith since it confirmed his true humanity and willingness to identify with humanity even in death. The crucifixion, Christians believe, showed the love of God at its fullest, in the death of the perfect man who was faithful to his own teachings to the end. Jesus died so that persons might see how far God's love for humankind would go. Christians believe that Christ's atoning act made possible the reconciliation of all persons with God. However, from the Christian view, the cruicifixion can never be understood without the resurrection.

3. Resurrection

Jesus was dead. He was taken down from the cross and was laid in the borrowed tomb of Joseph; a stone was rolled across the entrance. According to the account in the Gospels, the faith of his followers had also died. At Jesus' arrest, his disciples scattered and fled. Peter had been one of Jesus most ardent followers, yet when questioned in a courtyard near the trial, he denied that he even knew Jesus. Jesus' life had come to a sudden, violent, and tragic end. The disciples must have feared that neither Jesus' words nor acts were reliable, since hatred appeared to conquer the one who loved without measure and death had overcome the man who promised life eternal.

The disciples remained in hiding during the Sabbath day, sick with despair, doubt, and fear. On the third day after Jesus' crucifixion some of the women went to visit the tomb and found it empty, the stone rolled away. Then the cry was uttered by his disciples that was to echo through the centuries in the Christian community as the ultimate symbol of life and hope: "He is risen!" Despair changed to hope, doubt to faith, and fear to assurance. The good news that Jesus has risen from the dead created the Christian community and ultimately transformed it into the worldwide church. This gospel of hope and new life, which had convinced people of God's love through Jesus' life, now through the resurrection convinced people of God's power. For Christianity the irresistible message of the resurrection is that those who believe in Jesus can triumph over sin and even over death to new life. Viewed through the spectacles of faith, the resurrection allows Christians to see and understand the world in a new way. No longer can one quip that God either doesn't care or doesn't matter; in the resurrection of Jesus, God has given the ultimate sign of hope for eternal life.

The common elements of the five resurrection accounts in the New Testament (the four Gospels plus Paul's account in 1 Corinthians 15) are brief and the data meager. Three days after the crucifixion Mary and the other women found the tomb empty. Thereafter, it is claimed that Jesus appeared to Mary and to a few other followers. The resulting excitement and controversy are not about the events, but about what they mean. It seems beyond question that most early Christians believed that Jesus' body had been literally restored to life. This was proclaimed by men like Peter, who was later to become a martyr and die for his belief. It seems unlikely that Peter would give up his life for a fabrication or, even less, for an event based on a trick he had contrived. Even the New Testament records the false rumor spread by Roman soldiers that the disciples stole Jesus' body from the tomb (Matthew 28:11–15). This view of the empty tomb is still held by some persons today, but it misses the central meaning of the resurrection faith for Christians: how it changed the lives of those who believed Jesus had defeated the power of death.

4. Belief in Christ's Presence

The disciples, the authors of the Gospels, and Paul himself declared that the nature of their own experiences convinced them that Jesus was again with them. He had risen and was restored to the community as a presence that brought for every person the continued power of his love and a hope for victory over the consequences of death.

The historic accuracy of the accounts of the resurrection and the appearances of Jesus have been questioned, sometimes by biblical scholars. However, the variety and form of the reports are not so surprising if the authors were giving witness to how Jesus appeared to them in the light of individual experience. It would appear more contrived if the accounts were identical. Luke and John seem to affirm a physical resurrection of the body. Paul, in his first letter to the church at Corinth, probably our earliest account of the event in written form, reminds his reader that Jesus died and was raised "according to the scriptures." (1 Corinthians 15:4 KJV, NEB) Paul goes on in the same chapter, however, to argue concerning resurrection, "It is sown a physical body, it is raised a spiritual body." (1 Corinthians 15:44 RSV)

The disciples believed that this same Jesus who had shared their life was present to them again. So, after his death and resurrection, Jesus was reported by some to have eaten broiled fish with them (Luke 24:42), and to Thomas he showed the wound in his side inflicted by a soldier at the crucifixion (John 20:27). However, he was not always immediately recognized. In one account two of Jesus' disciples were walking on the road from Jerusalem to Emmaus. Jesus joined them and the three traveled and talked for quite some time. Only after the men invited Jesus in to supper and ate with him did they recognize him (Luke 24:13–31). The resurrection appearances were mysterious and unexpected.

Not all Christians agree about whether one is to understand the resurrection of Jesus literally or symbolically. However, most Christians clearly affirm their belief in the power of Jesus' resurrection. This awareness so affects the faith of the Christian community that it seeks to share its faith, its love, and its hope with all those who would hear. Christians have declared that whether or not Jesus' *body* actually rose from the grave that first Easter morning, no one could doubt his *spirit* came to life so as to transform the lives of his discouraged disciples in the first century and in the twentieth. Christians proclaim and believe, "He is risen."

The meaning of the life and love of Jesus, whom Christians confess as "the Christ, the Son of the living God," emerges in the story of his birth, crucifixion, and resurrection. Christians believe in an eternal life through Christ's presence that begins with faith now and continues to a future time when they shall share in Christ's victory over death.

The power of Christ's love and presence, which was so persuasive to the early band of disciples, led to Pentecost, the coming of the Holy Spirit, and the founding of the Christian church. It was this community of faith, or community of loyalty, which insured the historical development of Christianity. This segment of the Christian story begins appropriately with Paul who claimed to be filled with this Spirit. As the first great missionary and theologian of the church, he claimed to have acted not by his own power but by "Christ in me." The next case study, "Sacrifice or Service," is about a couple of young people who are struggling with what "Christ in me" means for their lives in very practical terms.

SERVICE OR SACRIFICE
Case Study B

For four years, ever since the time he entered college, Peter Murphy had planned to go into the Peace Corps when he graduated. Now the pressure was building up to take a different option.

Peter and Jane had married during the Christmas break of their senior year. Now with graduation only a few weeks away, Peter's father was hesitant about the Peace Corps decision. He had been very clear about including both Peter and Jane in his concern for their future.

"You and Jane need time to get settled and to get to know one another in your own environment without taking on the additional stress of learning to live in another country. Now that you are married you must assume an added sense of responsibility. A solid marriage is invaluable to both of you in order for you to be able to give your own talents to other people in need.

"Several companies have approached you, Peter, with solid offers which won't be there for long. With the summer experience you have had and your degree in business you are perfectly suited for a number of those jobs. If you leave the country for several years and are out of touch with the business world, it will be difficult to get a job on your return.

"Get a few years' experience behind you. Begin to get established. Then you can make a much more valuable and lasting contribution to those around you. There are always struggling businesses getting started that could benefit from sound management advice. This is a volunteer service you could give to your own community. You don't have to go half way around the world to help someone else."

Peter was clear that his father wasn't being sarcastic about his concern to help others. He knew that his father had served on the school board, that he was an officer in their church, and that his active in-

---

volvement in community affairs was a reflection of his own under-standing of the church.

Peter and Jane had talked about the decision for over a week. This past spring they had been to the Peace Corps "preliminary staging," and had a pretty good idea about what their work would be like. They had then both been accepted into the program, but they had to submit their response to Washington by tomorrow morning in order to be involved in the next training cycle.

Peter asked Jane to be as honest about her own feelings as possible. Her family had expressed some doubts about the decision, but Jane's response was clear. "We are mature enough to make up our own minds." However, she had expressed some uncertainty to Peter. "I'm very excited about traveling and seeing new places, but it would also feel pretty good to settle down for a while. I want most of all to teach school, but I'll be able to do that in either South America or the United States. Peter, you've got a much greater conflict about this than I do. To be content with the final decision, you really have to sort out what's most important for *you*."

Peter tried to summarize his feelings about his father's suggestions and his own reactions. "I have always had a deep sense of wanting to give what I could to someone in need. There's a great sense of satisfaction in that for me, but there's a lot more to it than that. The idea of 'loving your neighbor' doesn't make any sense to me unless I'm really committed to *doing* that. Where is the line between being responsible for myself, for *our*selves, and being responsible for other people? I've prayed about this and realize that basically the issue is getting my priorities straight.

"Right now is a time when we're not tied down by anything. It's a time when we're really free to give something of our lives and a time when we might change things to make the world a little better. I feel like I've been getting ready for so many years. But I can see some solid logic in what my father says. I really do need more experience. And I'm trying not to feel it would be a cop-out to my own ideals to be able to take his advice. I'm also aware that this may be a crisis for me because my father has just put into words some of my own doubts. I guess I'm trying to struggle with what I feel may somehow determine the future direction of our lives."

CHAPTER 3

Holy Spirit's
Presence and Power

From the Acts of the Apostles comes the dramatic story of the church's beginning:

> When Pentecost day came round, they [the disciples] had all met in one room, when suddenly they heard what sounded like a powerful wind from heaven, the noise of which filled the entire house in which they were sitting; and something appeared to them that seemed like tongues of fire; these separated and came to rest on the head of each of them. They were all filled with the Holy Spirit, and began to speak foreign languages as the Spirit gave them the gift of speech. (Acts 2:1–4 JB)

Men in Jerusalem from many different countries were attracted by the noise and said, " 'We hear them preaching in our own language about the marvels of God.' " (Acts 2:11 JB) Peter interpreted the meaning by the words of one of the ancient prophets.

> In the days to come—it is the Lord who speaks—
> I will pour out my spirit on all mankind.
> Their sons and daughters shall prophesy,
> your young men shall see visions,
> your old men shall dream dreams.
> ....
> All who call on the name of the Lord will be saved. (Acts 2:17, 21 JB)

Christians believe that the presence and power of this Holy Spirit of Christ, sent by God, changed a disillusioned and fearful band of Jesus' followers into disciples of Jesus Christ. In years to follow these disciples spoke and acted in such a way that thousands of people were persuaded to become participants in their community. This new people of God later came to be known as the church.

The community called the church still seeks to share with others the conviction that this Spirit of Jesus (the Holy Spirit, or God the Spirit) does make a difference. Christians are convinced that the Spirit can change the lives of persons and communities by making them freer, more loving, and at peace because they come to have real hope in an open and promising future. As seen through the Christian glasses of faith, the fullness of life is the gift of this Holy Spirit.

Mission of the Church

1. Reach Out to Those in Need

Christians understand the mission or assignment of the community called the church to come directly from Christ. The mission is to share Christ's love and life with others. The first test of Christians is not what persons *say* they believe, but what they *show* they believe. Being Christian is to be free in a special sense, trustworthy, loving, and hopeful. It is crucial to the Christian understanding that this response does not come out of fear, but out of love for God and for one's brothers and sisters. Quoting the prophet Isaiah, Jesus describes the task that many Christians now see as their own:

> "The Spirit of the Lord is upon me,
> because he has anointed me to preach good news to the poor.
> He has sent me to proclaim release to the captives
> and recovering of sight to the blind,
> to set at liberty those who are oppressed,
> to proclaim the acceptable year of the Lord." (Luke 4:18–19 RSV)

Christians believe that by the power of this Spirit they are called by Christ to share the good news and the good life with those around them. Specifically, many Christians are convinced they are asked to help other people in need and to share what they have with others to bring about today the situation described in the life of the early church in Acts: "There was not a needy person among them." (Acts 4:34 RSV) This is surely one of the underlying concerns for Peter Murphy as he tries to decide where and how he can best serve others.

Many Christians also interpret this mission or task as summoning them to act for persons who live in "captivity"—persons whose joy in living is "imprisoned" by loneliness, feelings of inadequacy, fear of failure, or the boredom of a meaningless life. Many Christians in community feel obligated to speak and act so as to bring hope to those who are in the darkness, blinded by hate or fear of persons different from themselves. Many in the Christian community have come to interpret Christ's message of love to mean working concretely, constantly, and consistently for the true freedom of those oppressed for reasons of race, poverty, sex, age, or other human conditions. This understanding of Christian mission was very important for some leaders who opposed slavery during the Civil War. This promise of liberation motivated many of those who have fought for the civil rights of minority groups, and it is a determining factor for some of those who struggle for the needs of the aged, the poor, and oppressed minorities.

2. Carry the Message of a New Covenant

For the church of the first century, the experience with the Holy Spirit of Christ was so decisive that the people believed that Jesus had fulfilled the promise of the kingdom of God. The early Christians were anxious to share this good news with others. In Christ's life, death, and resurrection the people had seen an example of God's rule in an individual life. For these and later Christians, renewed contact with Jesus through the Spirit offered what the kingdom had promised: life and love in all its fullness. So indeed, Christians might joyfully proclaim that this year, and every time and place since Christ's encounter with them, was the "acceptable year of the Lord" because a new covenant, a new relationship with God, had been established in Jesus Christ. This new covenant, based on God's love and faithfulness was to shape and direct the future mission of the church.

3. Where the Mission Fails

Unfortunately, but obviously, Christians and churches often fail to respond to or fulfill the mission which links them through Christ and the Holy Spirit directly with God the Creator. Christian individuals often speak and act in ways that are hateful, mean, and selfish. Part of Peter and Jane Murphy's struggle may be in dealing with the subtle, selfish desires for material wealth and security. From the Christian perspective, these desires are not in themselves sinful (breaking the link with God) unless they become one's *ultimate* concerns.

Historically the Christian church has often been more concerned with power and wealth than with service and charity. But failure, too, is a consequence of the God-created human condition of freedom. Sometimes a person simply feels compelled to be unloving, untrustworthy, unhelpful. In so doing, she or he may have betrayed the presence and power of the Spirit, but contact with the Spirit is not lost.

This failure can be compared to a bad connection in a stereo set. If the wires fail to make proper contact, the current does not flow. Rather than music that stirs and delights others, there is static and confusion. Those who anticipate music are understandably annoyed. However the record is not defective; nor is the instrument that transmits the message inoperative. The potential and promise are still present. What has failed is the connection. One experiences many faulty connections, but this does not negate the clarity or persistency of the mission for the individual Christian as a member of a community. Christians believe that the Holy Spirit enables the right connection—enables a person to be a participant and conductor in the orchestration of God's love to and for humankind. In the view of Christianity, faith and the power to share, serve, and heal are gifts of God through the Spirit.

Some may ask: How does one receive this gift of faith? Where does it come from? An analogy may be helpful here. Imagine a person at the bottom of a deep canyon. There is a strong rope hanging over the side of the canyon that reaches the bottom. If the person grabs hold, he or she can be pulled up over the side into the light of a new world. The person, however, has the freedom to decide not to take the rope. It may not look safe, or the world of the canyon may be sufficiently satisfying not to be worth the risk or effort. A Christian might see belief in Jesus Christ as the rope offered by God. Christians believe God gives them the courage or faith to take the rope via the Holy Spirit. But why some persons decide to take the rope (have faith that it will give them a new life) and some do not remains a mystery.

Saul Becomes Paul

Where might one glimpse the transformation, or the connection, in a person that brings freedom, joy, and hope? For many Christians this is a gradual process. For others it is a sudden, intense experience. Perhaps no biblical example is more dramatic than in the person and history of Saul, later known as Paul. His name was changed in the best covenant tradition of the Old Testament, like Abram and Jacob, as a result of an encounter with God which transformed his life. According to the Book of Acts, he was born in Tarsus of Cilicia of a Jewish family prominent enough to hold Roman citizenship. As a young man, Paul studied the scriptures in Jerusalem with Rabbi Gamaliel, one of the most famous and respected teachers of the day.

1. Persecutor of Christians

Paul described himself as a "Pharisee of the Pharisees." He was an ardent member of a Jewish religious party which stressed strict observance of the Mosaic law in all aspects of life, for example, circumcision, no work on the Sabbath, and not eating certain foods. Following Christ's crucifixion, Paul showed his zeal by persecuting the followers of Jesus as lawbreakers. He often traveled great distances to bring charges against these violators. The writer of Acts claims that Paul was present when Stephen was stoned to death for his repeated disrespect for the Jewish laws; Stephen had evidently declared his faith in Jesus as the promised Messiah. Remember that although the Romans were largely responsible for Jesus' crucifixion, the scribes (teachers of the Jewish law) and high priests had also rejected him; it angered them to have Jews proclaim that he was the promised Messiah. Paul may have participated in this violent event that made Stephen the first Christian martyr, or one willing to die for his faith (Acts 6–8). "Those who were scattered because of the persecution that arose over Stephen" traveled to Cyprus, Phoenicia, and Antioch. It was in Antioch that "the disciples were for the first time called Christians." (Acts 11:19, 26 RSV) This seems to be the first recorded instance of employing the term *Christ-ians* (literally "Messiah-folk") to the disciples of this crucified Jesus.

2. The Road to Damascus

On a similar trip to Damascus to arrest those Jews who followed Jesus and failed to follow the Jewish laws, Paul had his own decisive encounter with Jesus. This encounter brought about his conversion, literally, a "turning around" in his life.

The New Testament description of the actual event is minimal. According to Acts 9 there was a dramatic encounter in which Paul understood Jesus to appear to him in a vision, accompanied by such a flash of light and erupting with such a presence and power in Paul's life that it blinded him for three days. In the encounter Jesus identified himself as the one that Paul was persecuting and told him to rise and go into the city where he would be told what to do.

This encounter has been interpreted by some scholars merely as a profound, sudden awareness by Paul that caused hysterical blindness. An explanation of the details, however, overlooks the genuinely startling *meaning* of what this relationship involved for Paul's life and eventually for the history of the Christian community. Here was an event similar to the prophetic experiences in the Old Testament or to the resurrection appearances of Jesus to which Paul later compared it.

Paul was forced to wait for the recovery of his sight and to rethink his former ideas, values, and commitments. A brother in the Christian community named Ananias, who approached Paul with understandable fear, explained that he had been instructed to visit him so that Paul could " 'regain [his] . . . sight and be filled with the Holy Spirit.' " (Acts 9:17 RSV)

3. New Life in New Relationships

Paul came to understand the meaning of his encounter with Jesus as a result of his new relationship to the Christian community. Several days after Paul's meeting with Ananias and with other Christians, and with restored sight, Paul came to the very same Jewish synagogues where he had intended to harass the followers of Jesus. Paul now proclaimed this same Jesus to be "the Son of God." His sermons dwelt not on the details of Jesus' life but rather on the consequence of Christ's life and death. He spoke about the presence of Christ's Spirit for the fullness of life and about victory over death for men and women of faith. The chief persecutor had become first among the apostles. Paul understood *his* story to be an illustration, admittedly a dramatic one, of every Christian's encounter with this Jesus as Lord. The core of the Gospel was profoundly simple even for this most subtle of theologians: a relationship with God in Jesus Christ transforms the quality and direction of human life. This new faith in Jesus Christ (the "missing connection") changed Paul's values, commitments, and relationship to others.

The Church as Community

The encounter with Jesus also provided Paul with a vision of the church. As one Christian historian has said about Paul, to persecute the church was to persecute Jesus, and conversely, to serve the Lord was to serve the church. Christians came to believe that it was God's gift of the presence and power of the Holy Spirit which informed and empowered their own vision of the church. The first followers of Jesus understood that to be a Christian meant to establish a new type of personal relationship with God through Jesus and *also* to participate in a new fellowship of men and women who would be the instruments of God's activity in the world.

Being a Christian made it imperative that one also be a member of the Christian community. There were reasons of faith behind that basic conclusion. It was not simply that this small persecuted group needed one another for mutual support or desired to build up an organization called the church. The early church believed that men and women needed a loving relationship with one another to fulfill the promise of God's good creation.

There have been great individual contributions to the history of Christianity which Christians believe have resulted from direct encounters with God. Paul supplies a prime example. However, an interpretation of that experience depends on the function of others in a community. Paul learned about Jesus from Ananias and the disciples, as well as from the martyrdom of Stephen. Many Christians express their understanding of the church as a community by saying, "I become what I truly am only in relation to another person. It is impossible for me to respond to the promise of the gospel and gain life in all its fullness apart from community with other human beings. It is in my communication or sharing with you that I not only discover but fulfill my own identity, the sense of who I am and what I value."

For the Christian to have the fullness of life in isolation or loneliness is a contradiction in terms. It is also difficult for people to change very much without the support of others in a community. There are patterns of behavior which people often want to change: the tendencies to exaggerate, to be self-centered, to be overly sensitive to criticism, or simply to pretend they are brighter, more beautiful, more athletic, or sexier than they really are. It is almost impossible for people to try out a new style, however, if others still respond to them in the old patterns. It may be true that "all things can be made new"—but this must happen *slowly* and is possible only with help from other people.

The relationships we experience in encounters called friendships—relationships based on concern, caring, and loving—are examples of community or the communion of fellow creatures. The book of Acts reveals that the early church community tried to experience life based as much on sharing of one another's lives as on the sharing of bread.

Symbols of Community

1. The Vine

Christians believe that a faithful, loving, and hopeful relationship to other persons is dependent on a relationship with Jesus Christ. To communicate this, the early church used images or symbols they hoped would capture the imagination. The Gospel of John expresses through the image of the vine and the branches the intense dependency the early Christians felt on Christ and on one another. This biblical image coincides with our earlier picture of the tree of Christianity. Christ says, "I am the vine, you are the branches." The essential nourishment which flows through a vine to its branches enlivens them and enables them to bear fruit. In the same way the Holy Spirit "flows" from the resurrected Christ into his followers. This binds them together and empowers them with love for one another. Thus Christians understood Jesus when he said,

> "I am the true vine. . . . Abide in me, and I in you. As the branch cannot bear fruit by itself, unless it abides in the vine, neither can you, unless you abide in me. . . . for apart from me you can do nothing. . . . As the Father has loved me, so have I loved you; abide in my love." (John 15:1–9 RSV)

In his letters, Paul develops a second image for the community of faith: the body of Christ. The body, like the vine, is a living, dynamic image; there is a common life-giving source for all the active members and organs of the body. The parts of the body are obviously dependent on each other in order to give meaning and direction to the life it contains. The image also recognizes and celebrates the diversity of the members. So Paul compares the members of the church to eyes, ears, hands, feet, and sexual organs. Each is to be held in honor because of its indispensable function. "If one organ suffers, they all suffer together; if one flourishes, they all rejoice together." (1 Corinthians 12:26 NEB) Which part could one effectively do without and still be a whole, lively person?

In the same way the church has many members, all to be loved, respected, and cared for, because together they are the one body of Christ. In using this image Paul was always clear that the only true head of the body is Christ. Christians incorporate in this symbol of the body what they believe about life: persons are dependent on a relationship to one another and to Christ as Lord of the church and the world. Although Paul did not use the image, members of the early church came to speak of the Holy Spirit as the lifeblood of the church. They believed that the Spirit's presence and power surged through the community, giving it life and health.

The Christian community came to use both of these symbols, the vine and the body of Christ, in one of the central sacraments, or rites, of the church, known as Communion or the Eucharist (meaning "thanksgiving"). The heart of the Christian celebration became a common meal, following the pattern of Christ's last supper with his disciples before his crucifixion (Luke 22:14–20; Matthew 26:26–29). At this celebration Christians share bread or wafers symbolizing Christ's body. (This extremely significant sacrament is further examined in Chapter 7.) The sacraments of the Eucharist and of baptism, which marks a person's entrance into the church community, began to take shape in the New Testament and are mentioned frequently in the Gospels as well as in Paul's letters. Baptism and the Eucharist later became celebrations which strengthened the Christian community so that individuals could then go out and witness to their faith in the message of Christ. They affirmed Paul's declaration: ". . . though there are many of us, we form a single body because we all have a share in this one loaf." (1 Corinthians 10:17 JB)

The early Christians believed that the "body of Christ" was more than a metaphor. The human form of Christ had left the earth. But his love and work were to be carried on by the replacement for his physical body, the church, guided by the Spirit. Service, being for others, became one of the primary concerns of this early community. Christ had washed his disciples' feet as a servant (John 13). In being loyal to Christ's example, the community of faith was called to be a servant community, or a community of service and loyalty. Throughout the history and development of the church, the church has understood the scriptural themes of sharing and serving to mean sharing the gospel of Jesus Christ with one's words and life as well as serving people in need as if they were brothers or sisters. It is this understanding of the Christian faith that undergirds Peter Murphy's decision to spend his life in a form of service to other people.

The Great Commission

The desire to share and serve extended the servant community into a community of mission. Despite the positive and negative connotations which have grown up around the terms *mission* and *missionary,* these words mean a "sending out" with the authority and responsibility to perform a special duty. Christ's mission, according to Christianity, is the responsibility of *all* who are his followers. Though Peter and Jane Murphy might not be preaching or telling other people about Christ, they would show his love by their actions. By this understanding, they would be missionaries or those who share and serve because of their ultimate concerns.

Christians believe individuals are free to choose how and when they can best share and serve, as Peter and Jane Murphy are struggling to do. However, this sharing is not seen as an option; it is an obligation. This notion is rooted in what is called the great commission of Jesus, in which he instructs his disciples to go out and " 'make disciples of all nations.' " Christ's call, according to Matthew, is to baptize " 'in the name of the Father and of the Son and of the Holy Spirit' " and to teach people to observe his commandments (Matthew 28:19–20 RSV).

The first Christians claimed to experience the love of God. As this love dissolved their fears of death, guilt, and preoccupation with self, there was nothing which could stop it from pouring from them to other people and nations. Christians were convinced that it was this love which transformed persons and conditions; those who experienced God's love were anxious to share it. This love turned Paul around. He moved from a persecutor of the Christians to a servant and teacher of Christ's message. He went on three great missionary journeys in Asia Minor, Macedonia, and Greece. Against every kind of obstacle—flood, hunger, imprisonment, shipwreck, and beatings—Paul had as his sole purpose to share and serve.

Christianity Separates from Judaism

It is interesting, in light of Paul's vision of the church as a community and of his concept of mission as service, that following his conversion Paul did not go directly to Jerusalem to join the other disciples. Rather, after initially proclaiming his faith in Damascus, he withdrew for several years to prepare himself for his mission and to think through this new set of values and concerns (Galatians 1:17–20).

When he emerged from what is assumed was a period of study and preparation, Paul came out with a distinctive theology or way of thinking and talking about the gospel of Jesus Christ. Mr. Murphy argued for proper preparation for mission on Peter's part. Yet just when and how that preparation should occur is a matter of Peter's freedom of choice and how he understands God's will for himself.

A key idea in Paul's theology is freedom. Paul had found in the gospel of Jesus Christ a new sense of freedom for himself, and therefore for others, from the strict adherence to the details of the Jewish law. Remember, Paul had been a "Pharisee of the Pharisees," who previously imprisoned and persecuted those who failed to fulfill the law. There were Jewish Christians in the early church community concentrated in Jerusalem who believed all persons had to be Jews first and Christians second. These Christians wanted the new believers to be under the demands of Jewish law, such as circumcision and selected dietary restrictions. Paul thought this was nonsense; he declared that persons could not find their justification, their renewed relationship with God, through their own actions. In the Old Testament, God's people had offered many sacrifices to God to renew the convenant. Paul wrote that God had now sealed the covenant once and for all by the perfect sacrifice of his own son. Thus justification, a renewed covenant relationship with God, came only through faith, which was a gift from God.

For Paul to attempt to live by a code or a set of laws was not a genuine life at all. He declared that persons receive a full life in relationship to God through faith, not through the law. Paul wrote that faith and trust in God's presence can be prayed for and sought after, but finally they are gifts of God. Paul reminded both Jews and Gentiles (non-Jews) that even Abraham was justified by his faith in the promises of God. Paul believed that those promises were now fulfilled by Jesus Christ. Paul made this point of justification by faith by focusing on a covenant requirement for Jews—circumcision. Paul declared, "Since in Christ Jesus whether you are circumcised or not makes no difference—what matters is faith that makes its power felt through love." (Galatians 5:6 JB) Thus, from the Christian perspective, Peter Murphy would not make either choice because he was forced to, but because in his freedom he wanted to respond to others in love.

The result of cutting this legalistic knot, as some early Christians saw it, was to make the crucial break with Judaism and thus to become not a sect of the Jewish faith, but a distinct religious tradition called Christianity. Freed from the regulation of the Jewish community, this faith became available to the Gentile or non-Jewish world and eventually became an option for millions of people. Paul therefore played a crucial role in the mission movement and the dramatic growth of the church through a new interpretation of the faith. Yet Paul did not see this interpretation as a unique idea. For him this interpretation of faith was the obvious consequence of Christ's call to share with and to serve the whole world. Paul saw the power of the gospel as the answer to the law, the victory of life over death, in the person of Jesus Christ himself:

> For I through the law died to the law, that I might live to God. I have been crucified with Christ; it is no longer I who live, but Christ who lives in me; and the life I now live in the flesh I live by faith in the Son of God, who loved me and gave himself for me. I do not nullify the

grace [gift] of God; for if justification were through the law, then Christ died to no purpose. (Galatians 2:19–21 RSV)

Paul shared his message and tirelessly preached, taught, and organized new churches until he was arrested, perhaps on a charge of treason for claiming the Lordship of Christ in the realm of Caesar. Being a Roman citizen, he appealed and was sent to Rome for trial around A.D. 60, where, it is believed, he was executed. Paul was dead, but his message certainly did not die. The gospel of Jesus Christ, interpreted by apostles such as Paul, became a guide and standard for the growth of the church.

CHAPTER 4

The Church's
Growth and Guide

The claim that Jesus is Lord, based on the conviction that he brings life and love, has called Christians to share and serve in all places and conditions. There is now a worldwide church organization; there is continual reinterpretation of the gospel with a renewed theology for new times and situations; and Christian celebration has been adapted to fit vastly different countries and cultures. However, the source of the church's life is still Jesus and his apostles, the early leaders of the church. The pivotal period of history, when some of those who had known Jesus personally were still alive, came to be called the Apostolic Age; this period ended toward the close of the first century A.D.

Today most Christian churches still look on the New Testament church as the standard and guide for their life. This brief survey of the development of the history of Christianity will have a similar direction. The significant events in this history cannot all be named, and various Christians would dispute any writer's selection. A written overview of the development of Christianity since the Apostolic Age may be compared to a preview of a great historic film. The film would be about the history of the church; it is complex and contains many characters and several themes. In the preview the directors seek to expose only the basic plot and highlight some main characters with the expectation viewers will then want to see the film. The story portrayed in the history of Christianity is exciting and illuminating; but, of course, that is the judgment of the authors of this book and their perspective in selecting and interpreting persons and events must be taken into account. The bias of the authors is their belief that Christians in every age have seen the story of the church's struggle and growth as a resource of their own faith and a guide to their own actions.

Development of the Early Church

Despite the dramatic spread of Christianity following Pentecost and the witness of the disciples, Christianity ran into trouble, particularly from rulers of the Roman Empire which covered most of the known world. Some Romans came to regard their emperor as a god. Many Christians, however, refused to offer incense and homage to the emperor's image, an act Christians considered to be worship and therefore a violation of their basic commitment to Christ as Lord. Although Christians were generally obedient to civil law, they were considered by some Roman officials disloyal and rebellious to the state. Official Roman persecution began when Emperor Nero charged the Christians with setting fire to Rome in A.D. 64. The persecutions that followed were sporadic and localized but often fierce as crowds in Roman amphitheaters roared, "Throw the Christians to the lions." There were two periods of intensive empire-wide persecutions involving imprisonment or even death for some Christians. One came in the middle of the third century under Emperors Decius and Valerian, and the second was initiated by the Emperor Diocletian who, in A.D. 303–304, made an all-out attempt to crush Christianity. The intense efforts to stamp out Christianity evidence how powerful the church had become by the fourth century.

The first Christian emperor was Constantine, and he chose Christianity as a means of uniting the empire. He did much for the church including the establishment of the rights of Christians and making the Christian Sunday a legal holiday, but he also allowed the traditional Roman deities to be worshiped.

The spread and influence of the new faith was finally recognized later in the fourth century when Christianity was made the official religion of the Roman Empire. An interpretation of the life, death, and resurrection of Jesus of Nazareth by his first disciples had grown in about three hundred years to be the established religion of the most powerful empire in the world. Christians believed this had come about through the presence and power of the Holy Spirit as it touched Constantine and others like him. During the three centuries of sporadic but intense persecution and oppression, some Christians abandoned their confession of Christ, but many others remained faithful and hopeful.

As the church grew, there was a need for leadership and clarity about what Christians believed. Jesus Christ was seen as "Head of the Church His Body" and the ultimate source of authority. Church organization developed first at the local level with the selection of leaders known as deacons, elders, and presbyters. It was out of the latter office that bishops emerged. These new leaders gradually replaced the part-time traveling preachers with full-time clergy. By the third century regional disputes over matters of doctrine and practice were being settled by local councils of bishops. The church was generally organized with the same geographic divisions as the Roman Empire; higher authority was given to the bishops or patriarchs of the principal cities such as Rome, Antioch, Jerusalem, Alexandria, and Constantinople, which Constantine established as the new capital of the empire in the fourth century. Several of these metropolitan bishops were called pope which comes from a Greek word meaning "father."

The bishop of Rome claimed to be the first in authority among the bishops in matters of discipline and doctrine. He appealed to Matthew 16:18-19 to be the successor to Peter who had power and authority given to him by Christ. Many Christians, particularly in the Eastern part of the empire, resisted these claims by the bishop of Rome on the grounds that the authority of Peter was given to all bishops. Beginning with the barbarian invasions of the empire in the fifth century, Rome was cut off from the Eastern church and so the patriarch of Rome gradually established his authority and supremacy in the Western empire. Later the title "Pope" came to apply only to the bishop of Rome, the supreme head of the Roman Catholic Church.

Creeds Shape Belief

During periods of peace between the persecutions, the church was developing patterns of authority and leadership and was giving more definite shape to Christian belief or doctrine. The New Testament became the source of written truth, known as the canon (those specific books of early Christian writings accepted as genuine), and the bishops became the source of unwritten truth. However, disagreements developed among Christians. One group called the Gnostics (from a Greek word meaning "to know") considered this world, particularly the body, to be bad. If Jesus is good and the body is bad, he could not have had a real body. Jesus, they claimed, was not really born and did not really suffer and die as a human being.

The early church, partially in response to questions from groups like the Gnostics, set forth its beliefs in creeds. The word *creed* comes from a Latin word meaning "I believe." One such creed emerged primarily in the Christian West and was used as a statement of belief or faith for those receiving baptism, the initiation rite into the church. By the fourth century this confession of faith was secret and not to be recited outside the service of baptism and the worship of those faithful to the church. This creed served to reflect and shape Christian belief:

> I believe in God the Father Almighty, maker of heaven and earth,
>   And in Jesus Christ his only Son our Lord; who was conceived by the Holy Ghost [Spirit], born of the Virgin Mary, suffered under Pontius Pilate, was crucified, dead and buried; He descended into hell; the third day He rose again from the dead; He ascended into heaven, and sitteth on the right hand of God the Father Almighty; from thence He shall come to judge the quick and the dead.
>   I believe in the Holy Ghost [Holy Spirit]; the holy Catholic [universal] Church; the communion of saints; the forgiveness of sins; the resurrection of the body; and the life everlasting. Amen [So be it].

This statement of Christian faith came to be known as the Apostles' Creed, although it was not really written by the apostles. For millions of Christians in later centuries this creed, used by the early church centered in Rome, has expressed the central convictions of faith. It is used regularly today in worship and teaching. The Apostles' Creed stresses that God the Father was the "maker of heaven and earth," and thus the world must be good if God made it. Jesus Christ, his son, was actually born and suffered, which evidenced his genuine humanness. Jesus was really "crucified, dead and buried." All of these statements contradict the Gnostic teachings. Responding to other disputes the creed also states that the Father, Son, and Holy Ghost are worthy of belief.

The community of Christian believers, i.e., the communion of saints living and dead, is confessed in the creed to be a holy and universal church. The creed also declares that Christians shall be judged by God and may believe God's promise of genuine forgiveness of sins when one fails and confesses. Christians conclude by affirming that Jesus was not only raised from the dead, but that there will be a resurrection of their bodies and a life everlasting.

Councils of the Church

As the church grew and its faith and practice were clarified, major differences of opinion among Christians arose. The Emperor Constantine changed the capital of the empire from Rome to Byzantium, located at the intersection of Europe and Asia. He changed the city's name to Constantinople (which the Turks later named Istanbul). In the early centuries of the church the Christian East was richer and more populous than the West and was the center of theological controversy. One major argument between Christians was over the relationship of the Father, Son, and Holy Spirit. Christians agreed that they believed in only one God, but how was Christ related to God? Jesus Christ suffered and died, but he also rose from the dead, bringing everlasting life to those who believe in him. Christ must be more than a man; but if he is God then Christians would have two Gods, not one.

The quarrel erupted in Alexandria, Egypt, where an older priest named Arius declared Christ was more than an ordinary man but certainly less than God. Athanasius, a young priest in Alexandria, attacked Arius' views and said if Christ were less than God and more than man he would be neither. Athanasius declared that Christ as well as the Holy Spirit shared fully in the being of God. So Christ is God and the Holy Spirit is God. God is one, but within this One are three. This concept of God is called the Trinity and was worked out later in the church's life.

The dispute over the relation of Christ to God sometimes resulted in riots in which Christians ignored Jesus' demands of love. Constantine was shocked by the Christians' quarreling which he considered threatening to the unity of the empire. There was also at this same time serious disagreement about the date of Easter. In A.D. 325 in Nicaea near Constantinople the emperor assembled the first meeting, or council, of the whole church. In this dramatic gathering the swords of the empire were raised not to destroy but to protect the Christians they had earlier persecuted.

The Council of Nicaea debated the issues of faith and doctrine. Constantine was concerned with the peace and unity of the empire. On the advice of his theological consultant, he suggested the phrase "of the same substance" to describe the relation of Christ to God and make it clear that Christ was God. A local baptismal creed was revised to exclude certain Arian views (those of the priest, Arius), and the date of Easter was also settled. This council by no means settled all the difficulties. Debates about the relationship of Christ to God continued for many years. Other church-wide councils were called, such as the Council of Constantinople in 381, which issued a revised creed later known as the Nicene Creed, and the Council of Chalcedon in 451, which debated the relation between the divine and human elements in Christ's person. Bishops and priests were banished and restored, creeds were revised, and new doctrines emerged as the church sought to clarify its belief and to develop lines of authority on matters of faith and practice.

Scholars Interpret the Faith

1. Saint Augustine

Questions of faith remained central to the history of the church, and Christians returned again and again to the writings of Paul for insight. Such was the case with one of the most influential Western Christian thinkers in the first five hundred years of the church, Saint Augustine (354–430). Claimed by some to be the greatest personality of the ancient church, Augustine is also often considered a key figure by historians of this period. He is a hinge between eras.

Augustine believed his own life had been dramatically transformed by God's summons to Christianity—away from what he considered a self-centered and immoral life. He ultimately became the

Bishop of Hippo in North Africa. Augustine made significant contributions to the intellectual development of religious and secular history. Augustine's classic book *The City of God* interprets the change in history that occurred with the fall of Rome. He denied the claims of contemporary writers who blamed the fall on the Christian destruction of pagan worship and culture. Augustine wrote that greed was a motive for the Roman conquests; the barbarians were only paying Rome back for the way it had stripped others of their land. Rome would pass away, but other civil states would follow and the church would remain.

Augustine believed that God could intervene in the lives of nations and individuals. He saw human history as reflecting the struggle between good and evil. The earthly city, symbolized by Rome, represented the dangers of human society and culture. Over against this is the heavenly City of God, an expression of forces making for good. According to Augustine, the City of God finally will win in human history. Through the grace (or gift) of Christ, who is seen as the center, history is running in a straight line to God's goal: the establishment of a New Jerusalem that God's faithful followers will enter, and the ultimate triumph of good over evil.

Augustine's philosophy was a resource for understanding history that affected culture for the next thousand years. He knew persons needed governments and the church, but he wanted the government to be guided by the church. Later, popes sought to fulfill Augustine's dream of the City of God on earth. Dominant in medieval thought was the idea of relating everything people did, from pope to priest, and ruler to peasant, to the will of God in Christ. Therefore, much of Western culture was affected as people tried to live out the biblical theme, Christ is Lord of all life.

2. Saint Thomas Aquinas

God's will, or at least "goodness," did not always seem to come out on top, and it was hard for Christians to understand what God's will meant. Augustine had said, "Faith seeks understanding." But how was one to connect faith, belief in something not seen, and reason? An answer was offered by one of the greatest minds and most influential thinkers of the medieval period, St. Thomas Aquinas. The *Summa Theologica*, one of the great works of this thirteenth century theologian, is still used as a guide for Roman Catholics. Aquinas drew together the Greek philosophy of Aristotle, which contemporary scholars saw as a "new science" in conflict with teachings of the church, and his own understanding of scripture. He saw reason and faith not as contradictory or on two different levels, but as complementary, since both were necessary for a complete faith and a full life. Scholars could no longer easily confess "Christ is Lord"; they were expected to show where and how Christ was at work in the lives of individuals and nations. Thomas Aquinas, and others who thought as he did, greatly influenced education in Western culture. The idea of reason in dialogue with faith led the church to found schools and universities such as those at Paris, Bologna, and Oxford.

East and West Divide

When persons pray and reason together, they do not always agree. As the centuries passed, tensions grew between the church in the West, centered in Rome, and the church in the East, centered in Constantinople. The two branches of the church disagreed on organization, with the Eastern Church rejecting the bishop of Rome's claim to primacy; the East asserted that all the apostles were equal. The Eastern Church also proclaimed that interpretation of doctrine was not the exclusive right of the pope, but of all bishops in council. The bishops' interpretation, however, must be reflected in "the conscience of the church," which is the concensus of clergy and laity. East and West disagreed in emphasis on matters of faith and doctrine, with the Eastern Church placing more emphasis on the mystical dimension of all life and stressing Christ's resurrection. The Eastern Church leaders emphasized that the supernatural or divine world penetrates everyday life. Thus everyone—clergy and laity—should develop, through prayer and meditation, the capacity to experience directly God's presence. Finally, disagreeing in matters of worship and practice, the Eastern Church offered the cup of wine

(Christ's blood) as well as the bread (Christ's body) at Communion. The East also declared that a special role be given to icons or sacred images as symbolic representatives of divine persons, and that all clergy below the rank of bishop be allowed to marry.

In 1054 the Bishop of Rome excommunicated (banned from Communion) the Patriarch of Constantinople who responded with a similar action. Thus a major split, due to theology as well as differences in language and culture, occurred in the Christian church. The break was finalized in 1204 when crusaders from Western Europe on their way to Jerusalem plundered Constantinople.

The Eastern Orthodox Church today constitutes some 200 million members. Though worldwide, it is concentrated in Eastern Europe and the Middle East, with the Orthodox Church in Russia being the largest. The original division was based not only on political and geographic differences, but also on how the Gospel of Jesus Christ was interpreted in the style of life, worship, and action of the people. Yet the church in both East and West has also been aware of Jesus' concern for the unity of the church. Jesus had prayed that those who believed in him "may all be one." (John 17:20–26 RSV) When Pope Paul VI and Patriarch Athenagoras I met in Jerusalem in 1964, it was the first meeting of church leaders from the East and West since the split. This led eventually to their cancelling the mutual acts of excommunication made 910 years before.

The Power of the Church

The real power and influence of the Christian church in the West became apparent in the Middle Ages, A.D. 500 1500. Following the collapse of Rome in the fifth century, Western Europe was split into many different states, often at war with one another. The church, in the figure of the pope, often constituted the one strong authority. This led on several occasions to a conflict between a pope and a political leader such as Henry IV, the emperor of the Holy Roman Empire. In 1077 Pope Gregory VII challenged Henry on the questionable practice of the emperor appointing bishops. Sometimes these new bishops were men without religious training, and

they often were men who sought to be bishop for political or mone-
tary gain. Gregory asserted that the pope alone had the authority to
appoint a bishop. Henry refused to accept this decision. Gregory excommunicated him, expelled him from the church, and released all
his subjects from their feudal oaths of loyalty. Since Henry was dependent on the loyalty of his subjects, he came to Gregory during
the winter in the Alps barefoot and with a great show of penitence.
A compromise was worked out; religious authority in this scene appeared to conquer political authority. Popes following Gregory such
as Innocent III used excommunication and interdicts to control the
lives and actions of kings at the height of papal power in the thirteenth century.

1. The Crusades

The themes of authority and humility, of power and poverty,
stood side by side in the history of the church. Two quite different
movements developed during the Middle Ages, each drawing on
different understandings of the New Testament vision of the world.
One perspective was represented by the reign of the church over the
world.

The crusades of the eleventh to thirteenth centuries sought to
extend the authority and power of the Western Church beyond Europe. These military expeditions were often supported and encouraged by bishops who had as their alleged purpose ridding the
Holy Land, where Jesus had lived, of "the menace of Islam." The
quest to restore Christianity to lands then controlled primarily by
Moslems resulted in what most Christians today would admit were
instances of mercenary plundering and killing of people with different religious beliefs. Crusaders from many countries together captured Jerusalem in 1099, but they could not hold the city for long
against the Turks.

Authentic Christian zeal on the part of some crusaders turned
into human tragedy. When exaggerated or misapplied, this zeal violated the very foundation of the New Testament commitment to
love.

2. Monasticism Learns and Serves

Another perspective of some Christians in the early Middle Ages was to "get out of the world" and return to God. Men who sought to follow a strict religious life often became hermits and were called monks. Gradually they formed religious communities known as monasteries. Nunneries were established separately for women. Prayer, manual labor, and scholarship were the focus of this withdrawal from the world. In the fourth century one of these monks, Jerome, translated the Bible from Greek and Hebrew into Latin. During the later barbarian invasions the monasteries preserved learning and helped the church win over the non-Christian invaders.

In contrast to the violence of the Crusades a new form of monasticism developed in the thirteenth century in which friars (from a Latin word meaning brother) spent most of their time with people in need. Monastic orders such as the Franciscans and Dominicans sought to proclaim the gospel and to serve the people through teaching and caring for the poor and sick. The life of St. Francis of Assisi, the founder of the Franciscan order, demonstrates vividly the medieval church's commitment to and interpretation of the New Testament mission to serve under vows of poverty, obedience, and chastity. The monastic movement, which both safeguarded learning and brought service, stressed the early church's concern to be "*in* but not *of* the world," and to reform and purify the abuses evidenced in the church's desire for wealth and power.

3. Medieval Culture and Cathedrals

The church in the Middle Ages extended its influence to politics, economics, social welfare, and even art and architecture. One of the greatest examples of the influence of the church is represented in the magnificent medieval cathedrals. The church, like the cathedral which symbolized it, sought to tower above the world and draw the whole world in through its spacious doors so that all of life might show the glory of God the Creator and Jesus its Lord and Savior. Yet even at the height of the power of the church, there were abuses of power, vigorous advocates of reform, and a continual struggle over the "right" interpretation and application of the New Testament as a guide and vision.

Reform and Reorganization

Tragically in the eyes of some, and by God's providential or caring action in the view of others, the split between the Eastern and Western Churches was not to be the last nor even the greatest division in the once united Christian church. The Protestant Reformation of the sixteenth century was the beginning of the splintering of Christianity into the two major divisions in the Western Church, which came to be known as Roman Catholic and Protestant. Some 250 Protestant denominations and subgroups were to emerge by the twentieth century. Ironically, Martin Luther and many of the Protestant reformers did not originally intend to break off from the church, let alone establish a new church. Their hope was to reform the body of Christ by returning to the teachings and writings of the Bible as a guide to life and faith.

After the church had become one of the wealthiest and most powerful institutions in the Western world, it began to decline. During this period of history Europe was in turmoil with growing nationalism and disintegration of the old order. Bishops and kings fought over money and lands. In one of these conflicts the king of France captured the Pope and moved the papacy to Avignon under French control from 1309–1377. The invention of printing with movable type about 1450 soon made it possible to produce multiple copies of the Bible, the teachings of the church, and, later, the classic literature of Greece and Rome. The recovery of ideas from earlier literature led many readers to reevaluate the old patterns. Out of this Renaissance of knowledge and culture came scholars, known as Humanists, many of whom demanded reform in established institutions.

Scholars today acknowledge the need for church reform that had been urged prior to the sixteenth century by writers such as John Wycliffe in England; John Huss, a Czech; and Erasmus of Rotterdam, a great Catholic humanist scholar called "the Prince of the

Renaissance." These men declared that reforms were needed in the practice of offering religious positions, like bishoprics, to the highest bidder and selling indulgences, which claimed to free persons from all or part of the punishment after death for one's sins. Reformers objected to this practice of indulgences because forgiveness appeared to be bought, rather than being dependent, as Christ had promised, on feeling truly sorry and repentant for acts contrary to God's will and love. So many false relics were sold to raise money for the church that Erasmus claimed there were enough chunks of the "true cross of Christ" to build a battleship. Reforms were needed in church life where, contrary to the vow of poverty, many church officials lived in luxury; other clergy openly violated the vow of celibacy by marrying; and many clergy, some of whom had purchased their position, were so poorly educated they could not even read the Latin language in which the Mass or service of worship was written.

1. Martin Luther

Martin Luther (1483–1546), an Augustinian monk in Germany, hoped his famous Ninety-five Theses would stimulate debate and lead to eventual reform of abuses in the church. He posted these objections to current church policy on the door of the University Church in Wittenberg on October 31, 1517. Today, this date is celebrated as Reformation Day in many Protestant churches to mark its symbolic significance. Luther attacked the Roman Catholic Church, of which he was a member, not simply for the failures and abuses in church life, but because he believed there was evidence that the church had abandoned the "true faith" of the New Testament.

Returning to Paul's letter to the Romans, Luther claimed that Christians were "justified by faith *alone*" and thus could not be reconciled with God by indulgences or even by good deeds, but only by faith, which was a gift of Christ. Luther was also influenced by Paul's letter to the Ephesians:

> For by grace you have been saved through faith; and this is not your own doing, it is the gift of God—not because of works, lest any man should boast. For we are his workmanship, created in Christ Jesus for

good works, which God prepared beforehand, that we should walk in them. (Ephesians 2:8–10 RSV)

Luther asserted that good works were fine, if done willingly and for the love of the Lord and one's neighbors, but they had nothing to do with earning salvation.

Luther also insisted on a scriptural basis for the life of the church and individual Christians. He recognized only two sacraments, baptism and Communion, as founded in scripture. This was in opposition to the seven sacraments which had come to be recognized by the Roman Church. Luther insisted that each Christian should read the Bible as God's word and be guided to understanding by the Holy Spirit. To make this possible, Luther later translated the Bible into German (1534), thus affecting the entire culture as well as the standardization of the German language. He also insisted the worship service be conducted in the common tongue of the people, rather than in Latin, so all could share in "faith seeking understanding." Luther interpreted the idea of the "priesthood of all believers" by declaring that no priest or church officer need be a mediator or bridge between a believer and God. He said that Christ is the only head of the church and the one true mediator. Thus within this tradition, persons are to act as "Christs to one another" and reject the pope or any other person who claims to set limits to their understanding of, or access to, the power and presence of Jesus Christ.

The eventual result of Luther's protest saw the mixture again of religion and politics. Pope Leo X excommunicated Luther and declared him a heretic. Frederick of Saxony, a German prince, protected Luther. Other German princes in conflict with the power of the church called for reforms and thus provided the foundation for establishing the Lutheran Church, now one of the major Protestant denominations. Luther allowed priests to marry; he himself married a former nun, and they had six children. Estimates of Luther and his contribution vary. But whether he is seen as a reformer or as an enemy of the established church, he is recognized as a brilliant and dedicated man filled with strange contradictions as well as devotion and zeal to share and serve in the name of Jesus Christ.

2. John Calvin

Luther's writing and life released a new surge toward reform and opposition to reform which Luther himself could not contain. The movement to reform, to justify, and to revive the church according to the vision of the New Testament included the Calvinists and the Roman Catholic Society of Jesus. The work of the Frenchman John Calvin (1509–1564), whose views are reflected primarily in the Reformed or Presbyterian tradition, emphasized the sovereignty or rule of God. Calvin lived in Geneva and worked to develop a city government that sought to do God's will. Calvin's church, as well as the city government in Geneva, both ruled by elected representatives, are understood by many historians as factors which influenced the formative concepts of American democracy.

Calvin insisted on a strict style of life; he interpreted the Lordship of Jesus Christ as demanding faithful stewardship, or investment of one's mind, time, energy, and money to the glory of God. This disciplined and industrious interpretation of the Christian life was to have a great influence on subsequent generations and particularly on the values associated with capitalism. Calvin stressed the need for Christians to be good stewards, or caretakers, of God's creation. His distinction between flesh and spirit and his objection to worship aids not authorized in the Bible influenced the removal of paintings and statues from many Protestant churches and a move toward simple, unadorned church architecture.

Other church divisions sprang up in Europe, such as that initiated by Henry VIII in England resulting in the formation of the Church of England. John Knox began reforms in Scotland which shaped the Presbyterian tradition. Questions of faith and the proper interpretation of the New Testament church are often seen as matters of life and death, and many persons were imprisoned and put to death in the struggle between Protestants and Catholics.

3. Council of Trent

The Roman Catholic Church, realizing the great need for reform, developed what came to be known as the Counter Reformation. Seeing the actions of Luther and others as a misdirected

"Protestant Revolution," the Council of Trent (1545–1563) sought to defend and reconfirm some of the beliefs under attack. The council reaffirmed that all seven sacraments are to be seen as the means of grace (the way Christians are united with Christ) and that the Roman Catholic Church alone can interpret scripture. Numerous reforms were introduced regulating the issuance of indulgences and the veneration of saints or their relics. The method of appointment for bishops and priests was revised, and these men were directed to make closer contact with the people they were to serve. In 1542 the Roman Catholic Church also reorganized the Inquisition (originally begun in the thirteenth century) to punish heresy and return straying members to the church. While the sometimes arbitrary and cruel methods of the Inquisition are condemned by Christians today, the general drive toward reform by the church at this time was greatly aided by the formation of the Society of Jesus by Ignatius of Loyola in 1540. Known as Jesuits, members of this Catholic order have become famous for great learning, for the establishment of colleges and universities, and for missionary work in India, China, Japan, and South America.

Modern Quest for Religious Freedom and Unity

The end of the sixteenth century was characterized by conflict, competition between different Christian groups, and even religious wars, the wounds of which have not been fully healed today. Some persecuted individuals and groups moved to North America and other lands. In the seventeenth century the quest for religious freedom was a major factor in the age of exploration and discovery.

The division, conflict, and even competition between the different churches and denominations in Christianity called into question the true unity of Christ's body as stressed in Paul's image of the people of God. Perhaps more significant this conflict cast doubt on whether Christians, so splintered themselves, could be agents of love, peace, and service for others. In an attempt to heal some of the divisions in the church, Christianity in the twentieth century has produced the ecumenical (a reference to the "whole church") movement which promotes cooperation and unity among Christians. A fundamental part of this movement was the founding in 1948 of the World Council of Churches, based in Geneva, Switzerland. Though predominantly Protestant, this council has official observers from the Roman Catholic Church and full members from the Eastern Orthodox Church. The concern for church cooperation was encouraged by Vatican Council II called by Pope John XXIII. In many countries of the world—for example, India, Australia, Canada, and the United States—there have been consolidations of separate Protestant denominations at an increasing rate in the last few decades, as well as the establishment of national councils of churches.

Questions of Belief and Practice

The seventeenth, eighteenth, and nineteenth centuries ushered in the Enlightment and the Industrial Revolution that forced those within and outside the church to rethink their faith and values in light of new knowledge. There was a wider understanding of the universe as a whole and of its specific parts, through the testing of new theories by experimentation and research. These scientific advances demanded that Christians reinterpret and revise some ways of thinking and speaking about God and his relationship to humankind. Events such as the publication of Charles Darwin's work on *The Origin of Species* in 1859 in addition to intensive work in literary criticism of the scriptures drew into question the literal interpretation of the Bible, which had been held fairly universally through the Reformation period.

Questions now emerged: How does one reconcile science and religion? What authority does the Bible have and how is it to be interpreted as a guide to life? These issues are troublesome and challenging to Christians of the twentieth century who expect their faith to be alive and relevant for the daily events that confront them. However, careful examination shows that though the content of the questions is different, their form and focus are essentially the same as the questions which have encountered the person of faith during the nineteen centuries since the Apostolic Age. Basically, what does it mean to live and love from the perspective of Christian faith in God? How are Christians to respond to their brothers and sisters, their world and culture, their God and Lord in a faithful, loving, and hopeful way? These are issues of basic belief and practice—not only of Christianity but of all of human life seen through the glasses of faith. Peter and Jane Murphy are struggling with these same issues.

A biblical scholar has said that the New Testament is the case-study book of the early church. Paul, as well as every Christian since, has tried to apply his faith to specific decisions, to matters of life and death. The setting and historical development of the Christian faith can be understood as one resource to be drawn on as Christians analyze problems, make decisions, and take action about the cases or situations which they meet in everyday life. The church itself, as well as individuals within the church, has struggled with the problems of freedom and growth. This is highlighted in the following case about a family, but there may be parallel issues for the "family" of the church.

PART
II

Basic Beliefs
and Practices

FREEDOM TO GROW
Case Study C

Mary Johnson sat in the kitchen, waiting for her fifteen-year-old daughter, Katie, to come to breakfast. The night before, Katie's date, Mike Fedson, had been "picked up" on suspicion of drunken driving as he was bringing Katie home from a local high school club party. Mike was eighteen. He was taken to police headquarters and the couple with whom Katie was double-dating had brought her home at 3:00 A.M.

It was almost 9:30 when Katie walked into the kitchen. She told her mother she was sorry about worrying her so much the night before. Katie said she was afraid that if she had called from the police station, her parents would have been even more concerned. Mary was still quite upset and told Katie she was going to call the party chaperones. Mary reminded Katie that when she had agreed to let a fifteen-year-old go to this particular party with an older boy, she had been assured that no alcohol was allowed at the party. Mary told Katie that she was also considering calling a meeting of a number of the parents of the young people in Katie's crowd.

At this point, Katie broke down in tears. "Why do you want to embarrass me so much? It's not any of your business what the other kids do. That's up to *their* parents. I don't drink. I think it's stupid. But everybody else drinks and what I say about it wouldn't make any difference."

"Look, Mother. Mike had only a few beers in the parking lot. He wasn't drunk. On our way home the police stopped him to check on his license and they smelled alcohol on his breath. That's all. It's not so serious. We weren't in an accident or anything like that. You're blowing this whole thing up too big. If you call all my friends' parents and make a big thing out of all this, I won't have any friends left at all, and

---

for sure I won't have another date for the rest of my life!" Katie ran into her room crying and slammed the door.

Mary Johnson was still determined to call one of the adult chaperones for the club party and learn why drinking had been allowed. She finally called Ted Mallory who responded with cold, crisp logic. "My wife and I were asked to be present at the party, admit no alcoholic beverages, and generally supervise the kids there in the clubhouse. What went on out in the parking lot during that party was none of our business. This goes on at all the parties. You've got to give the kids some room to grow up. It's crazy to think about supervising them every minute. The seniors will be in jobs or in college in a few more months. It's better to let them learn to handle alcohol now than when they're completely on their own. We're forty-five miles from the state line. If we don't let the teenagers drink here, they'll drive into the next state where the legal age is only eighteen, three years younger than here, and get killed driving home. Come on, Mary, I know you and Bruce both drink socially. Why should it be different for the kids?" Ted Mallory hung up the phone with a definite "click."

Mary later said she really had wanted to tell Mallory off. "Sure, he was logical," Mary reasoned, "but the blunt truth of the matter is that letting those kids buy liquor is as illegal and irresponsible as Mike's driving when he had been drinking. I'm not trying to raise Katie in a cocoon, but kids need some clear limits until they are mature enough to make responsible decisions. Allowing them to break the law and slip around the rules isn't the way to go about it."

After the call to Ted Mallory, Mary sat back and tried to sort out what she saw as the options before her. She remembered that Katie's father had been equally disturbed this morning before he left for the office. He was quite angry with Mike Fedson and suggested that Katie should never be allowed to go out with him again. Bruce said to Mary at the time, "Maybe our decision to let Katie date a boy that much older or go to these club parties was a mistake after all. I don't know if Katie asked him not to drink or even if that would have made any difference. I want Katie to know that we trust her, but it's not fair to let her get into situations she can't handle at her age."

Mary was hesitant to tell Katie she could neither go to the parties nor date Mike anymore. Katie had been dating him for several weeks.

He was from a nice family and had always seemed courteous. Katie was just beginning to gain some confidence in herself, and to be perfectly frank, she seemed to be thriving on the special "prestige" of dating an older boy. Mary thought, "If Bruce and I tell Katie she can no longer see Mike, that could put a real barrier between us. Forcing Katie to see Mike in secret might turn into an exciting game that would be terribly destructive to her relationship with us. We've tried to give Katie more freedom than our parents ever gave us. But maybe Bruce is right. The old-fashioned limits might be the best thing for Katie.

"I guess what is *really* underneath the issue of Katie's dating is my wider concern for the whole crowd of teenagers who see drinking as a smart thing to do and who even manage to drink at organized parties where drinking is not allowed. I don't want to be the kind of mother who constantly interferes with her child's life, but I do want to do the most loving and responsible thing for Katie as well as the other youngsters involved. Maybe what out minister said at church last Sunday about the difference between real freedom and license and what it means to really love someone is at stake here. Wouldn't a meeting of some of the parents to talk over the issues be better than restricting Katie? Or would she be so hurt by my taking a step like this, that it would do more harm to Katie than good? What if I find out that it doesn't make any difference to the other parents after all?"

The hard logic of Ted Mallory and the sound of Katie sobbing in the next room made Mary hesitate before she started to look up the first number.

CHAPTER 5

Faith and Freedom

In a study of the beliefs and practices of Christianity, one might spend a great deal of time investigating the differences between various traditions. For example, those of the Quaker tradition and many who are Baptists accept no creeds or general statements of faith, and those who follow the Mormon tradition believe that there are two inspired books of God—the Bible and the *Book of Mormon*. However, instead of dwelling on these differences, this book seeks to expose some of the underlying concepts of Christianity. It is concerned with the roots and trunk of the tree of Christianity rather than its many branches.

Beliefs and Practices: Overview

The basic beliefs and practices of Christianity have been shaped by the setting and historical development of the community of faith, the church.

In Christianity, belief is linked with faith, but this should not be confused with the skeptical definition, "faith is believing what you know ain't true." Belief for a Christian is not based on wishful thinking but on experience—one's own experience as well as that of the Christian community. Christian beliefs are expressions of a relationship of faith. To say "I believe in . . ." means "I know and have trust in someone or something." Belief or trust depends on a meeting or encounter with a person or object. For Mary Johnson to *believe in* Katie implies that a special kind of relationship has been built between them based on knowledge of each other, trust, and past experiences.

Part I of this book has provided a preliminary survey of the Christian experience as recorded in the Bible and in the history and theology of the church upon which Christians draw for their basic beliefs. This is what is meant when one says that the setting and history of Christianity are the *resources* which form and inform Christian commitment (belief) and action (practice).

The word *practices* refers to actions which are performed regularly. A practice not only gives evidence of a belief or commitment, but it also intends (1) to increase learning or proficiency, (2) to apply knowledge, or (3) to reflect a relationship. For example, (1) practice on the piano increases keyboard skills; (2) the practice of medicine makes use of medical skills to bring about healing; (3) the practice of being more loving is the reflection of a relationship to a person or a group of persons that depends on a certain knowledge and skill. Christian practices contain all three of these dimensions, with the emphasis on the third. The specific Christian practices discussed in the following chapters are prayer, ethics, and worship. The practices depend ultimately on the experience of a person's relationship with God and neighbor.

According to most Christians, regular prayer increases the meaningfulness of addressing God, heightens one's sensitivity to hear God, and strengthens the relationship with God. Practice in decision-making may be called ethics, if it is informed by Christian beliefs and commitments. This kind of reflection increases one's knowledge of the criteria for loving and responsible action. Christian ethics is based on a loving relationship with God and neighbor and is made possible by God's gift of freedom. Finally, many Christians agree that the meaning of *worship,* i.e., an act which shows one's reverence for God, or devotion, is deepened by both frequency of worship and understanding of one's commitment or faith in God. The discipline of worship reflects the Christian's relationship to God and to his or her brothers and sisters in Christ.

Beliefs and practices also result in change, both of the self and of the community. The test of beliefs, and the practices which accompany them, is the way they are enacted or carried out. Beliefs can change one's life and the lives of others so that they form the basis of a lived faith and practiced commitment.

Part II of this book examines the ways in which faith and freedom (Chapter 5) and love and hope (Chapter 6), the core values of Christianity, inform the basic practices of prayer, ethics, and worship. The practice of worship, which emerges from the core values and is acted out in patterns of celebration (Part III), is considered more thoroughly in Chapter 7.

The Core Value of Faith

1. Faith in God

The most fundamental belief in Christianity is faith in God as Creator, known as Father, Son, and Holy Spirit. The Apostles' Creed, the most universally affirmed of any Christian confession of faith, begins, "I believe in God the Father Almighty, maker of heaven and earth. . . ." Faith in God is indisputably accepted by Christians.

Faith, which was identified earlier as one of the central Christian values, has been called, along with love and hope, one of the Christian virtues. It has often been interpreted differently by Christians and has different meanings even in this text. The word *faith* is used to refer to the Christian faith as a historic religion and is frequently used as a synonym for Christianity. For some Christians, faith also implies a special religious experience such as the feeling of being saved (feeling reconciled or "at one" with Jesus Christ). Sometimes faith refers to knowledge or belief in propositions or doctrines of the church such as those expressed in the Apostles' Creed. When one uses the expression "from faith to faith" to describe how the Christian story has been handed down from one generation to the next, then faith is used in a manner that encompasses all these uses of the word and reflects the diverse aspects of the basic relationship.

The disciples said to the Lord, " 'Increase our faith.' " (Luke 17:5 RSV) Jesus reminded them of the power of the gift of faith with several stories. Later, the disciples and Jesus encountered a blind man beside the road who called out, " 'Jesus, Son of David, have pity on me.' . . . [Jesus replied] 'What do you want me to do for you?' 'Sir,' he replied, 'let me see again.' Jesus said to him, 'Receive your sight. Your faith has saved you.' And instantly his sight returned and he followed him praising God. . . ." (Luke 18:35–43 JB)

For the blind man in this story, faith refers to the relationship he had with Jesus. The man so trusted Jesus' power that he expected to receive his sight. The relationship was grounded in what he had heard and come to believe about this person Jesus and the God in whom he believed.

Faith describes a special kind of relationship between persons or between groups. In the Western tradition a relationship of faith has often been one of trust, belief, and confidence. Therefore, to say "I have faith in you" means "I trust you," "I believe in you," or "I have confidence in you." There is another element of faith, however, that emphasizes the dynamic, two-way nature of a genuine relationship. Faith also requires loyalty. A faithful relationship suggests a certain performance with certain responsibilities required if it is to continue to be a faithful relationship. Consider the relationship between Mary and Katie Johnson. Why do you think a two-way faith is important for a genuine relationship between this mother and daughter?

Faith as trust or loyalty is at the core of the Christian understanding. What Christians specifically mean when they use the word faith is belief in, and knowledge of, God, Jesus Christ, and the Holy Spirit. Faith in this context emerges as *unconditional* trust and loyalty, the ultimate concern by which a person and community live.

This does not mean that Christians are never in doubt. Even one of Christ's followers cried out, " 'I believe; help my unbelief.' " (Mark 9:24 RSV) It is very difficult for Christians always to have the same level of faith in God's love or the same type of relationship in the midst of tragedy and suffering. Sometimes it is even difficult to believe in God at all. But without trust and loyalty the relationship between God and humankind is threatened.

There is a story of a farmer in Oklahoma who had a huge watermelon patch. Each night someone took one of the farmer's melons. The farmer devised a plan to stop this nightly practice. He put up a sign which read: Beware: One of These Watermelons Is Poison. The next morning the farmer walked out and did not see any evidence of loss. He was feeling very pleased with the strategy until he got around to the front of his new sign and noticed it had been slightly altered. It now read: Beware: Now Two of These Watermelons Are Poison. An act of unfaith, evidence of not trusting, may "poison" a relationship. This is true in either a relationship between persons or between an individual and God. Acts of unfaith lead to distrust and suspicion.

When this happens, Christians believe that one's hope for the future is threatened.

Christians through the centuries have been convinced that God always remains faithful; it is persons who break the relationship by being untrusting and unreliable. As a result, according to Christianity, a person without faith in Jesus Christ loses the fullest possible life and loses his or her "true self" in the bargain because both the relationship to God and to other persons is undermined. Thus even in times of doubt and uncertainty, Christians seek to remain faithful by developing patterns of prayer, worship, and the application of Christian values to daily decisions.

Faith in God basically depends on some understanding of who God is; this is evaluated by the relationship between God and those who trust him. It is important to say "some" understanding, since for Christianity there is a mystery about God and his creation that cannot be penetrated. Mystery, however, does not mean that nothing can be known of God, but only that not *everything* can be known. What the believer does know of God is what has been revealed through personal experiences, through the scriptures, through prayer, and through the community of the church.

2. Faith in a Good Creation

The first words of the Bible and usually the first words of a confession or creed concern the Creator and creation. Virtually all Christians agree that God is the Creator and that this creation is essentially good, but Christians have many different opinions about the method of creation. Some see the creation as one dramatic pronouncement of God's word at a specified time and place; others believe in the gradual and mysterious process of continual creation sometimes described as evolution. (See Chapter 1.)

It has been suggested that if one rightly understands what the Bible means by God as the Creator, he or she has rightly understood the whole Bible. This remark emphasizes the conviction that God the Father, by his free act, is the origin of life and the world as we know it. The amazing thing from the Christian view is not that God exists, but that the world exists. It is in the story of the creation of life that humankind comes to know that God is personally related to each creature.

This judgment depends on one's experience in the world—whether negative or positive.

A father and son were decorating a Christmas tree. As the son, who was six, put the star on the top of the eight-foot tree, his father said, "Jump down from the ladder and I will catch you." The boy was reluctant and afraid. So the father urged, "Don't you trust me?" Finally the boy jumped and just as he was about to reach his father's outstretched arms, they were pulled away and the boy crashed to the floor, shaken but not injured. The boy's father responded. "That will teach you not to trust anyone." And it did! In contrast to this experience, the Christian would say that he or she has experienced God's faithfulness, even if God chooses to "catch" the children of creation in very different ways.

Christian theology (which is an orderly way of thinking about Christian belief and practice) claims that persons rightly understand creation only when they come to see it as including personal creation and the foundation of a relationship with God. This is a covenant relationship which anticipates trust, loyalty, and obedience. By grace, God continues to create, to give the source of life, as his free gift. *Grace* is the word that Christians use to describe God's gifts to them. Thus, from the Christian perspective, God's creatures are dependent on him for their life, freedom, and capacity to love. Human freedom and love are an imperfect mirroring of divine freedom and love. According to the Christian, there is a gracious power of God present in the created world, despite failures and disasters on the part of humanity. One can point to evidence of God's gifts in the fullness and vitality of life, in the beauty and creativity of nature and persons, and in the sustaining sources of food and companionship that make life possible.

3. Faith in Human Worth and Dignity

Faith in God's good creation provides the basis for the Christian belief in the dignity and worth of every human being. One goal of Christian faith is to enhance the quality of all human life by responding to God in faithfulness and loyalty. The form of that response is clear in the commandments of Jesus and was affirmed by Paul in his letter to the Galatians: " '. . . love your neighbor as yourself.' " (Galatians 5 : 14 RSV) The commitment of Christian theology is not to value mere biological survival. Mary and Bruce Johnson are not simply concerned about Katie's "survival." In thinking about both Katie and her friends, Mary seems concerned about the quality of their lives and the values they develop.

Christians believe the scriptures deal with the quality of human life and with relationships between people. This understanding of the meaning and direction of human life emerges out of faith in God's good creation. This all sounds quite beautiful and idyllic. However, observation of people's lives discloses obvious problems.

Sin and the Problem of Evil

Evil cannot be avoided or ignored in life or faith. A glance at the newspaper or one's personal history reveals the pain, death, ugliness, and frustration that emerges from failures, accidents, crimes, famine, tornadoes, or war. Christians view evil differently. Some understand it as part of God's creation which has a meaningful purpose. They see good taking its meaning only in relation to evil. Thus one is able to recognize good only in contrast to evil, beauty to ugliness, fulfillment to frustration. Others see evil as a direct result of the freedom granted by God to his creatures. In the exercise of this freedom, humankind corrupts the intended goodness of God's creation but does not destroy it. Finally, some Christians believe evil is an independent adversary of God and describe this as a force, as the Devil, or Satan.

Though evil is understood in different ways, most Christians see evil as subordinate to God and thus maintain that God's creation at its core is essentially good. God's creatures are to be respected and loved while his creation is preserved and protected. The creation story does not provide a full explanation of the purpose and function of evil or of God's plan for the meaning of life. Human understanding is limited; human vision is too narrow to "justify" sin and evil. Thus most Christians understand the poetic account of the Garden of Eden in Genesis (Genesis 2:46–3:24) to acknowledge the existence of evil and sin in order to show how they affect God's good creation and the quality of human relationship with God and neighbor.

The forbidden tree in the garden leaves no doubt that a "right" relationship with God is one of trust and obedience. The forbidden tree represents the authority of God as Creator but it also represents his love for his creatures. Human beings, though viewed as being created "in the image of God," are not puppets. They possess a will and are responsible for the decisions of willful choice. There is no freedom without genuine choice, no obedience without a recognized request, and no good response without a less acceptable alternative. "Good" is a value judgment in relation to that which is considered evil.

As an Old Testament scholar notes, the symbol of forbiddenness—the tree—is located "in the midst of the garden," not at its outer edge. This reflects the belief that the decision of the human will is never a side issue; a choice between obedience or rebellion is always at the center of human existence. Freedom and responsibility are the central qualities of human life in terms of faith in God as Creator. Decisions (on matters of good and evil) depend on, and are affected by, relationships of authority and love.

1. Sin Distinguished from Evil

Sin is a much loved activity and a greatly misunderstood word. Sin is a narrower notion than evil. Christian theology usually restricts the use of the word *sin* to acts or situations that involve the whole person, especially acts of will. One scripturally based understanding of *sin* is that of having "missed the mark." (1 Timothy 6:21 RSV) This suggests there is a target, or goal, which Christians recognize and consider a worthy aim. Sin can also be described as "breaking the laws of God." Many Christians interpret the Old Testament Ten Commandments (Exodus 20:1–7) as valid laws of God. These rules establish a standard or pattern for human behavior. When Jesus was asked, which of these ten was the greatest commandment, his disciples report that he replied, to " 'love the Lord your God with all your heart, and . . . your neighbor as yourself.' " (Matthew 22:36–39 and Mark 12:28–31) Thus Christians interpret as sinful any act which does not reflect love and which thus separates humans from God. Christians see sin as much more than missing goals or breaking rules. They see a tremendous power in sin that so penetrates the world with self-serving interests and the attempts of one person to use others to meet his or her needs that Christians have called sin the sickness of the world.

2. Sin as Separation

Sin is often identified only with particular acts and associated with breaking a conventional norm such as the excessive consumption of alcohol or irregular sexual activity. However, this popular connotation "misses the mark" of the *central* understanding of sin in the Christian tradition. Specific acts (for example, murder, theft, cruelty, and dishonesty) may be judged sinful, but these acts are not themselves identical with sin. Sinful acts are only the consequence of a person's whole attitude and will.

For example, as a result of an argument with his wife, a man got unjustifiably angry with his children who interrupted their conversation. He yelled at the children and even punished one of them. His words and actions toward the children were wrong and could even be judged sinful. However, the real problem was the distorted relationship with his wife.

For Christians sin in its core meaning refers to an attitude or quality of relationship. Sin is an attitude that distorts or endangers a person's relationship to God and, as a result, his or her relationship with neighbors. A person acts toward God in rebellion rather than obedience, with deception rather than trust, with self-preoccupation rather than concern for others. He or she may act in an unloving, untrusting, and oppressive way with other persons. However, these acts are judged sinful primarily in relation to God's standards of love, trust, and freedom.

In the Christian view the concept of sin provides a way to understand how human beings "miss the mark" and fall short of what God created and expects. In the same way, children sometime fall short of their parents' expectations, and vice versa. Katie disappointed her parents because she came in quite late, causing them to worry about her. Mary and Bruce Johnson had expected Katie home on time and believed that there would be no drinking at the party. Bruce is worried that Katie and Mike are not yet responsible enough to be allowed more freedom. On the other hand, Katie expected her parents to be understanding. She feels that she had done nothing wrong. Katie may feel that her parents do not trust her and her friends enough to let them develop their own limits.

3. Sin Described as Pride

Christians have described sin, this attitude of the whole person, in many different ways. One of the most important definitions, according to theologian Reinhold Niebuhr, is "pride." Pride does not mean obvious exaggerated self-esteem or bragging, but rather that subtle, often disguised inclination of all persons to overestimate their importance, powers, and achievements.

There is a folk story about a frog who hated to see the birds fly south every autumn to a warm climate while he remained in the cold north. One day the frog approached two geese and asked them if they would fly him south. The birds were glad to help but did not know how to manage the trip. There seemed to be no way they could carry the frog. The frog devised a marvelous plan. He took a piece of rope and put one end in the mouth of each goose. Then the frog grasped the middle of the rope in his mouth so he could be carried along. They had been airborne about ten minutes when the trio flew over a cornfield. A farmer looked up at the sight and said, "I wonder who thought of that!" The frog answered, "I did!" As he did so, down he plunged to the ground.

When a sense of pride dominates everything one does, one tends to disregard other persons and even uses them to achieve one's own interests and goals. Sin for Christians is "playing God the Creator" with themselves and others. This attitude of pride distorts or diminishes the freedom and worth of others. If someone succeeds in "using" or "playing with" another person's responses and feelings, the freedom and worth of both have been reduced.

4. The Role of Repentance

There are moments when persons who understand the world through the Christian perspective become aware of their pride and seek to change the relationship between themselves and other persons. It is in a person's attempt to restore the full relationship to God that he or she acknowledges sin. In the Christian tradition this is called confession, when one acknowledges this separation, or repentance, when one expresses sorrow for an action or attitude. Repentance is a practice which results directly from a Christian's belief in the relationship between God and oneself.

If a friend breaks his or her word to you, you no longer have confidence in that friend's word. However, if the individual comes to you and says, "I'm sorry," this would work toward healing your broken relationship. Your honest response of "That's all right" can then bridge the gap between you. Mary and Katie Johnson may be able to restore a trusting relationship only when they both say "I'm sorry" and begin to listen more carefully to one another.

The Christian community believes that God's son established patterns of loving relationships. Then when Christ died, the relationship between humanity and God was confirmed. This was God's act for humankind. The human concept of confession—of saying "I'm sorry"—is an acknowledgment of separation from God. As one theologian has said, "To confess your sins to God is not to tell him anything he doesn't already know. Until you confess them, however, they are the abyss between you. When you confess them, they become the bridge" (Frederick Buechner, *Wishful Thinking* [New York: Harper & Row, 1973], p. 15). The Christian believes this act of repentance is made possible through the accepting love of God in Jesus Christ. A Christian understands this acceptance as forgiveness. One then becomes free from pride and selfish goals and can respond in love to other persons. Christ instructed his disciples. "When you shall stand to pray, forgive if you have aught [anything] against any man; that your Father also, who is in heaven, may forgive your sins." (Mark 11:25 DB)

As a practice, repentance (1) is an act in which Christians seek to understand themselves better; (2) is an application of the knowledge that, through Jesus, God continually loves and cares for individuals; and (3) reflects the desire on the part of the penitent (the person confessing) to restore the right relationship with God and with other persons.

Belief in the Holy Trinity

The great mission for every Christian is described in the Gospel of Matthew as, " 'Go therefore and make disciples of all nations, baptizing them in the name of the Father and of the Son and of the Holy Spirit.' " (Matthew 28:19 RSV) This biblical passage is the origin of the Christian belief in the Trinity, which means "three." This belief maintains that while there is only one God (thus preserving monotheism), God is at the same time three different persons: Father, Son, and Spirit. Thus Christians confess their faith not only in God the Father as Creator, but also in God the Son and God the Holy Spirit.

1. God the Son

As a summary of previous sections, especially Chapter 2, which discussed Jesus, a Christian could say that it is in and through Jesus Christ, in the account of his life, death, and resurrection as confessed and interpreted in the New Testament, that persons come to know more fully who God is and what God's relationship to humankind is meant to be. Christianity declares that Jesus has shown what it means to have faith in God even to the extent that he was able to sacrifice his own existence by laying down his life for others. Christians encounter in Christ a person who was genuinely free and loving. He not only shared the fullness of life in his own person, but served and transformed others as his life and love enhanced the quality of their lives. Christians believe, however, that Jesus is more than a guide for life; as he is both divine and human, his death and resurrection bridged the gap between God and humankind. On the grounds of the testimony of the community of faith and affirmed by personal experience, Christians came to believe that this same Jesus, described and responded to in the Bible, was Lord and Savior. He was therefore "truly God" and to be confessed and followed as God the Son.

2. God the Holy Spirit

Jesus proceeded to affect and change communities and thus individuals through the power and presence of his Holy Spirit, or Holy Ghost, following the time of Pentecost. (See Chapter 3.) This Spirit healed, comforted, encouraged, judged, and saved the relationship between God and humankind, thus shaping the quality of human life. The fullness of life promised by Jesus came to be seen as a gift of the

Spirit. It is perhaps obvious that Christians confess this Holy Spirit to be God the Spirit.

3. The Triune God

The concept of the Trinity is difficult to comprehend and has always been interpreted by the Christian community as a mystery. The belief was not officially formulated until the third century A.D. and was intended more as a confessional summary of Christian faith about God than an explanation. The importance of this unique Christian concept seems to be in showing how one encounters the power and presence of God through three dimensions. An analogy has been suggested for the Trinity which compares it to an artist's creative act. First comes the artist's *creative idea* in which one imagines the entire work before it is painted; this can be compared to the image of the Father who encounters humankind in his continual creation. Next is the *creative energy* which is the working out of the idea in space and time with sweat and passion; this is the work of God incarnate, the divine Son. Finally there is the *creative power* which is the response the work of art draws from those who see the painting and are attracted or grasped by it; this is the indwelling or presence of the Holy Spirit. The point is, these three are one; no single part could be considered the whole work. None of them functions without the other. The analogy intends to convey the Christian concept of the richness and complexity of understanding God's identity and the power and diversity of his interaction with humankind.

Christian Prayer

Mary and Katie Johnson need to talk to one another and communicate their feelings before the tension between them can be resolved. In much the same way, Christians believe that a way is needed to keep alive the covenant relationship with God the Father, Son, and Holy Spirit and to seek guidance concerning what it means to be faithful, loving, and free. Prayer, perhaps the most common Christian practice of all, is the means by which Christians realize this communication.

Prayer often employs forms of address which suggest a loving and responsible relationship between a parent and child. Perhaps the most significant prayer in Christianity begins, "Our Father. . . ." It is simply called the Lord's Prayer. Matthew reports that Jesus taught these words to his twelve disciples as a model for prayer. They draw together the promises of God's love in a response of faith:

> Our Father who art in heaven,
> Hallowed be thy name.
> Thy kingdom come,
> Thy will be done,
> On earth as it is in heaven.
> Give us this day our daily bread;
> And forgive us our debts,
> As we also have forgiven our debtors;
> And lead us not into temptation,
> But deliver us from evil. (Matthew 6:9–13 RSV)

Prayer in the Old and New Testaments is a spontaneous response to God, who is personally related to the one praying and thus can be addressed as Father. As in human relationships, if contact is broken, if sharing ceases, then the relationship dissolves. Jesus taught his disciples to use an intimate form of address and to ask God for the things that were crucial to them: God's presence with them; essentials of life such as daily bread; forgiveness and the grace to forgive others; and the faith to maintain hope when one is tempted by doubt to sever the relationship with God.

Christians believe they are to pray "in Christ's name," thereby ruling out all selfish requests and the notion that prayer is a kind of magic that will catch God's attention. The essence of prayer for a Christian, one scholar suggests, is not asking but offering, not self-seeking but self-dedication. Jesus' own prayer to his Father—" 'not my will, but thine, be done' " (Luke 22:42 RSV, KJV, NEB)—summarizes this idea. The children of God are expected to be concerned with other members of the "family." A Christian is expected to pray for others in need and to translate his or her concern into helping, healing, and compassionate action. This essential concern for others makes Christian prayer communal in character even when it is done privately. God is not simply "my Father," but "our Father"; God's concerns are everyone's concerns.

Faith lives on prayer. The statement "Faith is nothing but prayer" emphasizes the crucial role of prayer in the Christian life. Christians live out their faith in communication with both God and neighbor; they are always linked to both, in love, by God's act of creation. The Christian may pray in adoration (love), confession (repentance), thanksgiving (praise), and supplication (requests). Meditation is also understood by many Christians to be a form of prayer in which one seeks to be quiet and listen to God. The practice of prayer seeks to maintain and renew in freedom the covenant of wholeness for oneself and others.

Christian Freedom

The concept of human freedom is closely related to the Christian understanding of the covenant relationship between God and humanity. The Christian belief in freedom is important not only because it can lead the believer to certain practices but because it influences the attitude with which a Christian does certain things.

Movements for liberation or freedom from oppression based on race, color, creeds (both religious and political), and sex have as great an influence on society today as at any time in recent memory. Women's liberation and black liberation are only two examples of the value placed on freedom. Different church bodies have interpreted liberation in different ways, and those involved in the liberation movements have seen organized Christianity as both oppressor and liberator. It would be generally agreed by Christians, however, that the New Testament gospel is a gospel of freedom.

In the discussion on repentance it was noted that the Christian can become free from pride and selfish goals and can respond in love to other persons. The Christian believes he or she becomes free before God and for others.

1. Freedom from Self

Christianity, which stresses personal transformation that results in a new sense of freedom, has an ironic contradiction at its foundation. Paul reminds Christians of their freedom when he speaks about circumcision:

> Christ set us free, to be free men. Stand firm, then, and refuse to be tied to the yoke of slavery again. . . . When you seek to be justified by way of law [being circumcised in order to fulfill the Jewish law], your rela-

tion with Christ is completely severed: you have fallen out of the domain of God's grace. For to us, our hope of attaining that righteousness [reconciliation with God] which we eagerly await is the work of the Spirit through faith. . . . . You, my friends, were called to be free men; only do not turn your freedom into licence [complete permission] for your lower nature, but be servants to one another in love. For the whole law can be summed up in a single commandment: "Love your neighbor as yourself." (Galatians 5:1, 4–5, 13–14 NEB)

Here Paul connects the concept of freedom in Christ to the idea of being a servant. To become the servant of Jesus Christ and thus servants of one another is the clue to authentic freedom. How can servanthood be the key to liberation?

Christianity declares that the relationship of faith or trust in God, which is nurtured by prayer, makes one a free person, subject to none. This trust means that a person is free from worry and the concern to live up to some inner drive imposed by one's parents, one's culture, or one's own self-centered ambition. The Christian faith promises freedom from guilt, from inappropriate regret, and from the fear of death. Christianity assures the believer of God's forgiveness and urges the forgiveness of neighbors to liberate one from the bondage of past failures and mistakes. The promise of eternal life, to be examined in the next chapter, frees the Christian from the anxiety and dread connected with one's own death and the death of those one loves. The freedom granted by God is not simply a freer mind or a new attitude toward life and death. Christians believe that Christ's actions, his death and resurrection, have changed the relationship to God and the reality of the world in which one lives.

The New Testament declares, "If God *be* for us, who *can be* against us?" (Romans 8:31 KJV) One is also free, according to Christianity, to make a decision about the use of one's time, energy, talents, and resources, whether that be a vocational choice to serve the needy, hungry, and oppressed of the world or to share one's resources and gifts with other persons and communities. Many interpret the gospel as declaring that the believer is also free from human authorities and legalistic rules that restrict and oppress the essential human freedom of oneself and others. This conviction has often made the gospel the foundation of movements for liberation. However, this freedom is not license to harm others or to live irresponsibly within a society. Paul warned, "do not turn your freedom into licence. . . . ." The promise of the gospel under the guidance of faith is also put well by Augustine: "Love God and do what you want." God's love and guidance keep a person's freedom from turning into the license to infringe on the rights and freedoms of others for the sake of personal gain. In the case study Mary Johnson considers the Sunday sermon on freedom and license. How do these concepts apply to Katie and Mike's situation?

2. Freedom Before God

It is important to stress that Christian freedom is not primarily freedom *from* but rather freedom *before* and freedom *for*. It must be admitted that at times the covenant community of the church, particularly when it was under pressure or attack, has mistakenly stressed "freedom from" and has added its own slavery in the form of rigid dogma, behavior restrictions, and even the oppression of others who were not Christians. (Recall the Crusades, the Spanish Inquisition, or even the burning of "witches" in Salem.) However, history has usually judged these actions to have been overly zealous and often distorted interpretations of the gospel.

Christians believe that God created persons for a relationship with him, but God also granted freedom of choice in matters of life and faithfulness. This means the freedom to obey *or* rebel. A relationship with God is not that of a slave but of a free servant. The covenant relationship is one of creative and loving dialogue; people are responsible *before* God for commitments and actions but are not *forced* to fulfill what is required. A person must determine, with the support and advice of the covenant community of faith, what love demands and how to respond. Freedom *before* God carries responsibility and liberation.

3. Freedom for Others

Freedom *for* others is certainly a core declaration of Christianity. Christianity believes and expresses, as seen in the interpretation of the crucifixion and resurrection discussed in Chapter 2, that Christ took up his cross and laid down his life for humanity. The gospel message proclaims that to serve those who are hungry and poorly clothed, as well as those who are lonely or threatened, is to serve Christ himself. (See Matthew 25:34–45.) There are many loving people who are not Christian who do things for others. However, it is the concept of Christian freedom through Christ's love which makes the Christian's attitude and *reason* for acting for others distinctive. Ideally the Christian seeks to help others because of an overflowing love for them and not out of guilt, or fear, or hope of salvation. According to Paul, to be servants of one another—by giving help in the form of kindness, friendship, constructive criticism, or forgiveness, and by affirming the essential dignity and worth of human beings—is to be truly free. To be committed to values that give priority to being "for others" is at the core of the Christian gospel.

The application of Christian belief in God's good creation (interpreted through the practice of prayer) to a life that gives daily evidence of being free for others is the test of Christian faith. Christian beliefs become "lived," and freedom becomes real only through the love of God and his assurance of eternal life.

CHAPTER 6

Love and Hope

At the turn of this century, an American physician who was a Christian went to live with a community of people in the Nile Valley of Egypt. He experienced a sense of closeness and commitment among these people which he had not previously known. Here he also found a tragic situation: the villagers were always sapped of energy, there was widespread anemia, and no amount of food or medicine seemed to help. Most of the people did not die immediately; they wasted away. The physician was one of the first to identify the cause of the affliction as a liver fluke that appeared to thrive in the silt of the Nile River.

There was no known medication to rid the people of this parasite. The doctor decided to return to the United States to John Hopkins Medical School, where he had once studied, in order to seek a cure. He got as far as Ellis Island, in the shadow of the Statue of Liberty. The U.S. immigration authorities told him that under no circumstances would he be allowed to come into the country with the tiny vial of flukes essential for his medical research. The dilemma left him with an impossible choice: should he return to Egypt where there were no adequate research facilities, or should he go on to John Hopkins with its medical scholars but without the essential flukes? He thought about the consequences. Then, in the restroom on Ellis Island, he slowly took the lid off the tiny bottle of flukes. However, rather than emptying the bottle into the sink, he poured the contents down his own throat. He then carried the deadly flukes into the country in his own body. This man so deeply loved his "brothers and sisters in Christ" that he was willing to take on their crippling burden of a slow death in order to search for a cure.

The underlying theme of Chapter 5 was faith in God. To continue the analysis of faith, love, and hope as central elements in the Christian belief, this chapter now turns to a discussion of love. Perhaps a clearer understanding of the concept of Christian love will help explain the motivation of this Christian doctor. It may also help explain what it means for Mrs. Johnson to act in a loving way toward her daughter, Katie. How might Katie express both her love for her parents and her own need for freedom to mature?

Christians respond in love because they understand that God first loved them. This becomes evident in the life, death, and resurrection of Jesus Christ, whom Christians believe lived the ideal life of love. For a Christian to respond to a "demand of love" means to act in as loving and responsible a way as possible with God and one's neighbor. This is the summary of Christian commitment.

How does one know what love demands in a particular situation? The response to this question involves an understanding of what Christian love means, as well as the practice of Christian ethics.

New Testament Concept of Love

The author of the first letter of John declares:

> God is love; he who dwells in love is dwelling in God, and God in him. This is for us the perfection of love, to have confidence on the day of judgement, and this we can have, because even in this world we are as he is. There is no room for fear in love; perfect love banishes fear. For fear brings with it the pains of judgement, and anyone who is afraid has not attained to love in its perfection. We love because he loved us first. But if a man says, "I love God", while hating his brother, he is a liar. If he does not love the brother whom he has seen, it cannot be that he loves God whom he has not seen. And indeed this command comes to us from Christ himself: that he who loves God must also love his brother. (1 John 4:16–21 NEB)

The New Testament repeatedly describes how persons formed and maintained loving relationships with one another and with God because they knew this Jesus Christ. As incredible as that sounded to the people of the first century, or may sound to people in the twentieth, Christians have believed that this same Jesus was the key to a full or complete life. Jesus' own lived faith illustrated and dramatized what Christians were to value. He directed them to their ultimate concern: a loving and faithful relationship with God and neighbor. But what seems even more incredible was that these Christians in the early church reportedly gave evidence of this faithful relationship in renewed and transformed lives. These men and women began to help "those who were in need," which is a Christian definition of *neighbor* (see Luke 10:29–37). The early Christians lived out their faith until others outside the Christian community exclaimed with respect, "See how these Christians love one another!"

The basis for this renewed covenant in the early Christian community was a transformed life. The deciding mark of a follower of this Jesus Christ was not what one said but what one did, not what one publicly confessed but how one acted toward neighbors—family and strangers, friends and enemies. Relationships were more important than universal principles; a lived confession was more significant than a spoken creed. Christians believed in the quality of life and relationships as the ultimate test of what one really valued.

In Matthew, Jesus told a story which illustrates that love demands Christians to help those in need. In this parable Jesus is addressing the people: " 'For when I was hungry, you gave me food; when thirsty, you gave me drink; when I was a stranger you took me into your home, when naked, you clothed me; when I was ill you came to my help, when in prison you visited me.' " The people then asked, when did they see the Lord or when did they do these things for him? He answered, " 'I tell you this: anything you did for one of my brothers here, however humble, you did for me.' " (Matthew 25:35–40 NEB)

Jesus gave Christians the primary example of sacrifice for others in his own style of life. He associated with outcasts, which alienated him from "accepted" society. He gave up any hope of financial security and lived at the most minimal level of his day. In his continual ministry to others he showed his deep love for his "neighbor." Jesus gave Christians a model for applying a loving relationship to God in specific situations: he forgave a woman taken in adultery (John 8:1–11); he drank water from a Samaritan woman despised by the Jews (John 4:1–30); and he visited and healed those who were sick (Mark 1:34; Matthew 8:16; Luke 6:17, etc.).

Modern Interpretation of Christian Love

But how do Christians today respond to the demands of love? How

do they apply their beliefs to situations that were not specifically addressed in scripture? These situations might involve vocational choice
(as in the second case "Service or Sacrifice"), parents setting limits for
their children ("Freedom to Grow," the third case), or conflicts created
by modern medical advances ("Dance of Life," the next case study).

Christian belief and practice are matters of creative and faithful
interpretation by the members of a community, informed by the resources of their history as well as by the presence of the Spirit. The
church is not only a community of faith but a community of interpretation. The criterion for interpretation and action is the same today as in
the time of the New Testament: What does love, informed by and
grounded in God's love, demand at this moment in life?

Christians would say that love itself needs to be reinterpreted in
succeeding generations and situations if followers are to have a lived
faith. Love was considered by Paul to be the central Christian value:
". . . the greatest of these is love." (1 Corinthians 13:13 RSV, JB)
However, in the mid-twentieth century, love is often associated with
romantic affection or sexual gratification. It is quite clear in the story of
the American doctor in Egypt that the Christian virtue of love is
neither vague nor sentimental.

Over the centuries thousands of books and statements have been
written to interpret Christian love. Two of the most insightful guides for
a modern understanding are H. Richard Niebuhr and James M. Gustafson, both professors of theology, who base their interpretation on the
many biblical references to love and loving as well as on their own
experiences. Try to relate the following descriptions of love, based on
the writings of these theologians, to your own personal experience.

Love is rejoicing in the presence of the loved one. Love is reflected in
attitudes and actions which show genuine joy when someone we love is
with us; this means joy in everything that makes him or her great or
glorious. Love rules out jealousy or resentment that makes us want to
match adventures or accomplishments with a friend or enemy when
they are appreciated and loved more than we are. Christian love is
basically optimistic and leads one to celebrate the essential goodness of
God's creation and the happiness of one's fellow creatures.

Love is gratitude for another person. It is the declaration "I love you"
without the hidden implication "when you become what I want you to

be—in three years or thirty." Love accepts a person as he or she is, without making that love conditional on change or improvement. Love as gratitude means that we recognize our dependency on the skills and wisdom of others. We can be supported by the activity and affection of others whom we may not even know well. Yet gratitude must be guarded by respect so that it will not deteriorate to uncritical loyalty. When we fail to appreciate and respect, we fail to love.

Love is reverence. At the same time one draws near to a person or community, it is also necessary for that person to keep some distance. Intimacy may be desired by a person but it is also accompanied by a need for privacy. Any attempt to absorb the one loved into your own life or to use him or her for your own interests is the rejection of love. In the same way, you deny real love when you identify with someone you love so much that you lose the distinctiveness of your own person and your own diversity. As reverence, love seeks to know other persons not out of curiosity or desire, but rather with a profound unwillingness to violate their integrity. In the wider community, reverence means a basic respect for individuals, groups, or nations. Disagreement, dialogue, and evaluation are not excluded from love as reverence. Rather, reverence seeks to protect the integrity and distinctiveness of other persons, groups, and nations to shape their own future, to determine their own values and priorities. To deny respect is to threaten love.

Love is loyalty. This involves faithfulness to, and defense of, the person and commitments of the ones we love. This faithfulness is not apart from constructive criticism, but love falls short if it does not recognize the commitments and causes for which the loved one is ultimately concerned. Faithfulness also includes forgiveness. Christians believe that someone with real love does not continue to punish or hold a grudge against another who has hurt or failed them. Jesus teaches that one should forgive not seven times, but seventy times seven. Thus the Christian tries to respond time and again with acceptance. Forgiveness of another person is a recognition of God's love and loyalty, because God continues to accept and love us even when we fail to follow his example of love.

Christians believe that there is no love of God apart from love of neighbor. If we say we love God, while hating our brother or sister, we reveal that we are liars. Thus loyalty to one another is essential for our life as a community. Faithfulness is the structure by which love is expressed. Love cannot be faked or forced from the outside; it is an inner motivation that gets demonstrated in a continuing commitment to others. A lack of loyalty results in the absence of love.

Katie's parents must express their love for her in a creative way that respects her integrity as a maturing young adult. Love requires a willingness to listen and establish direct and open communication. Responsive love calls for the assurance that Katie's parents trust her and will continue to support her even when she makes what is in their view, a mistake in judgment. Genuine love involves a mutual commitment by parent and child which declares, "I love you because you are *you* and not because of what you do to me or for me." The loving relationship modeled in Christianity is constant in its support and willing to take risks for the sake of others.

Can the fullness of life exist without rejoicing in the presence of others? Without gratitude, reverence, and loyalty for others, without the love of God and neighbor concretely enacted, the hope for a more fully human life characterized by freedom, love, and peace remains unfulfilled for the Christian community. The question of how love gets enacted or applied focuses on one of the principal practices of Christianity: ethics.

Application of Love

1. The Basis of Christian Ethics

Suppose a Christian is making a decision: to have an abortion or not, or to recommend that action to a friend; to sacrifice a lucrative job offer in order to serve in the Peace Corps now, or wait until he is more experienced and financially secure? A Christian may face the decision to set limits for someone, or trust that person enough to set her own limits, as in the case of Katie and her parents. A Christian may be faced with a threat to his own life with the possible hope of helping others in need, as the doctor who took on the disease of his friends. There are also times when a Christian must decide simply whether to tell the truth about how he or she feels about any one of these decisions or to conceal, even lie, about his or her judgment to family and friends.

If you were facing a problem, on what grounds would you decide?

This is the situation of *ethics*. If the person making a decision is a Christian, that decision is the context for Christian ethics. Action is most often unavoidable. Even a decision not to decide affects you and others. It was stated earlier that religion has to do with an ultimate concern, with a way of valuing. A particular religious belief concerns your faithfulness or loyalty to someone or something. The Christian religion involves faith in and loyalty to God as known in Jesus Christ. The standard or guide for a Christian decision is the "love of God and neighbor."

2. Ethics Distinguished from Morality

When commitments conflict and it is important to make a decision, how do our values, our ultimate concerns, help us to analyze the situation and act more responsibly and creatively? It is important here to distinguish between ethics and morality.

Morality applies to day-to-day activities which are guided by mores or accepted patterns of activity. Despite the current charges of a loss of morality in government, business, family life, and education, most people are moral. They obey the laws and conventional patterns of society. Most pay their taxes (though some fudge on items in their tax return). Most people in our society refrain from directly harming or persecuting others as in child abuse or murder, though there may be oppression of minorities or women regarding equal access to education, jobs, or housing. People usually do not steal or stuff ballot boxes, (except occasionally through an exaggerated insurance claim or in local precinct elections). In other words, the majority of persons in our society are moral, and, according to our standards of behavior, provide the security for the society to function adequately, if not as well as one might wish.

Ethics, on the other hand, primarily refers to a *process* of thinking and deciding about priorities, about what we value and why. Ethics is not like morality which affirms and follows conventional patterns of behavior. Ethics demands that we be equipped to reflect on human responsibility for our actions, in light of what we value. Jack Stotts, a Christian ethicist suggests, "Ethics for Christians is a process of examining our moral lives (or our immoral lives, if that applies!) in light of our commitment to Jesus Christ, in order that we may be more faithful."

Simply put, Christian ethics asks, "What ought I to do in this situation as a person before God and for others?"

3. Resources for Christian Ethics

Although there are many ways of interpreting Christian ethics in the history of the church, ethics does not mean giving "answers" or providing set "rules" for right conduct. There are, of course, rules or guides, such as the Ten Commandments (Exodus 20:3–17) or the Sermon on the Mount (Matthew 5:1–11), that come from the Bible and are interpreted in history. The church has also tended to provide "answers" to some ethical questions. However, Christian ethics has emphasized in recent years that ethical decision-making is a response to God's love at particular points in the lives of persons and communities. Values and commitments of individuals and groups change and old patterns give way to new ones. So it is an over-simplification to say that the practice of Christian ethics is finding the right rule and applying it to oneself or others.

Dietrich Bonhoeffer, a German pastor who was executed in a Nazi concentration camp for resisting the new "mores" of Hitler's Third Reich, noted, "An ethic cannot be a book in which there is set out how everything in the world actually ought to be, but unfortunately is not." Christians believe that ethics must be an intensely honest and practical analysis of the conflicts and decisions that shape one's daily life. In scripture and tradition the accounts of God's radical involvement with men and women in moments of conflict and decision show how Christians have made decisions. Paul declared faith in God's presence when he made the decision to preach rather than persecute; John Wesley, who founded the Methodist Church, and Mother Teresa, a world famous nun who has established a new Catholic organization to serve the sick and dying in the slums of Calcutta, are both examples of persons who made decisions based on their understanding of a relationship to God and to other persons. Many Christians believe that prayer, as well as these historical and contemporary resources, can help them understand and respond in a more faithful and loving way to those situations that demand a decision. But a clear "answer" may never be provided. Indeed, two *different* responses to a decision about abortion, a vocational choice, or the mode and quality of living may *both* be faithful and responsible.

4. Consequences of Christian Ethics

The goal of Christian ethics is not to provide "the Christian solution," even if that could be determined and if all Christians were to agree. Rather, the aim of ethics is to clarify the standards, motives, and consequences of an *individual* decision in light of faith and trust in God's love and justice. The purpose of Christian ethics is to assist Christians in understanding "what" they value and "why." Then they may act with consistency and integrity to apply that value in their relations with others. The practice of Christian ethics is the living out of "faith seeking understanding." Paul describes the practical outcome of ethics in his letter to the Galatians as "faith working through love." (Galatians 5:6 RSV)

Christians believe that in one's personal life a crucial effect of faith in God is freedom from both pride and fear. Thus the central consequence of the love of God and neighbor, as practiced in Christian ethics, is a life which is more loving and therefore more fulfilling and responsible to God and humankind. Christians believe there is a quality of joy about serving in love that is greater than the surface gaiety of personal gratification; this joy can change the quality of one's whole life. A Christian's relationship with God, which means the regular practice of a loving response to those in need, is like infectious laughter that grows and spreads. We cannot always account rationally for its origin or its spread, but we can see the benefits of this kind of joy. The Christian life takes seriously the difficulties, obstacles, and tragedies of existence. Joy is profound because it can endure pain and suffering. The mark of Christianity is not superficial happiness; rather it is a willingness to cry with those who cry and be glad with those who are happy. If Christian ethics is the practice of responsible decision-making (remembering that "responsible" has its root here in the sense of "responsiveness" to God and humankind), then the love of God and neighbor is the practice of the fullness of life.

5. Ethics as a Part of Christianity

If responsible and loving ways of believing, deciding, and acting are at the core of Christianity, then is the practice of Christian ethics not the same thing as Christianity? As one scholar of comparative religion has noted, it is a fatal error to make ethics the essence of any religious belief. Religion often involves the "summons" or call to a high standard of human conduct. In Christianity, however, one's eyes must not be focused on the summons but on the vision that makes this call both understandable and possible. For example, in a home a young child does not ask, "How shall I behave?" as much as "How will I feel if I fall below my parents' expectations?" Or, as a teenager might respond, "Boy, would my mom be mad if I did that!" The ultimate question, or the vision is one of relationship. How do both parent and child remain faithful to a relationship that increases love, freedom, and fulfillment for both of them? This is the question which faces the Johnson family.

This Christian vision is not only of a responsible relationship between individuals and God; it is also a communal vision. It is difficult to make decisions alone. The Christian often feels he or she can come to a responsible answer in conversation with others in the community of faith. The community of the church is considered by Christians as the recipient and interpreter of the covenant with God that guides responsible relationships.

Christians consider right action a by-product of one's relationship with God and other persons. This may be overstating the case, but in all the variety of Christian interpretations, saying that faith is the same as ethics would be rejected by most Christians as too narrow. If we concentrate on ethics we may lack the sensitivity and flexibility of faith as *trust*. Then we would lose confidence in an open future promised by *hope*. Hope is the topic of the next section as well as a central theme in the final case.

Christian Belief in Hope

Following Faith and Love, Hope is the third of the great values of Christianity to be considered. Hope is at the core of Christian belief and practice; it is even maintained by some Christians that to be without hope is to reject the Christian faith altogether. For the Christian hope makes faith reliable and makes love meaningful.

With no hope, a Christian could feel bound by the fear of making a wrong decision. Hope implies a special kind of trust and freedom crucial to the concept of fullness of life. The Christian doctor introduced at the beginning of this chapter was led by his deep love of the people suffering in the Nile Valley to drink the vial of deadly flukes. But he was given the strength to make this crucial decision through the *hope* that he might find a remedy.

Paul affirms in his letter to the church in Rome:

> Not only the creation, but we ourselves, who have the first fruits of the Spirit, groan inwardly as we wait for adoption as sons, the redemption of our bodies. For in this hope we were saved. Now hope that is seen is not hope. For who hopes for what he sees? But if we hope for what we do not see, we wait for it with patience. . . . We know that in everything God works for good with those who love him. (Romans 8:23–25, 28 RSV)

At the Johns Hopkins medical facilities between 1913 and 1923, the pastor-physician withered physically for ten years as he pursued and finally found the cure that allowed him to return to Egypt and the community for which he had taken the risk and the mission. He had had no assurance that he would not fail, but for this Christian, *hope* made his act of love meaningful.

What does the Christian mean by hope? Christian hope does not mean hoping for a sunny day during the vacation next week, hoping for an easier examination next month, hoping for a greater profit next year, or even hoping for the disappearance of world hunger in the next decade. Hope has sometimes been confused with a happy-go-lucky "Pollyanna" attitude toward life that ignores the realities of human dissapointment, suffering, and injustice. Superficial optimism about the present or, more self-deceiving, a narcotic hope of a future paradise where all wrongs are righted and all suffering compensated for, is not a true or full picture of Christian hope.

Most Christians would say that ideally hope should be understood as a real anticipation of a new day, a new possibility for living, a sense of the fullness of life as we experience it now. Hope can be confidence that the future is genuinely open. But this type of hope is based on experience, not on fantasy or wishful thinking. This kind of hope makes a difference in how a person lives and responds in the present.

1. Hope Influences Commitments and Actions

What persons hope for affects what they value, what they live for, what they desire from day to day, what they say, what they do, and finally, who they are. For example, what you expect in the future often determines why you practice the piano or your tennis serve, how you apply yourself to studies or the practice of law, how you cultivate a relationship with a new friend and how you practice loving. All of these are conditioned, if not determined, by your hope and expectation for the present and for the future. Authentic hope gives direction to one's present activity and does not stop with simply fueling the imagination.

There are, of course, radical differences in what one hopes for. Hitler had a hope for Nazi Germany, and Martin Luther King had a dream for America. As in the case of followers of Hitler, however, putting hope in a person, a cause or a community which degrades the human goal and encourages injustice or oppression can have disastrous effects. Hope in another person, cause, or community may touch those involved with compassion, courage, and conviction that can change human history. Many believe that Martin Luther King's vision for equality and justice through the Civil Rights movement embodied this kind of hope. Many of the founders of the United Nations had a dream for world peace, and William Booth, the founder of the Salvation Army, had a vision of caring for society's outcasts.

The opposite of hope is despair. Despair brings with it a hopelessness that makes action now or in the future meaningless. It is like the desperate sign on a subway that says, "Help," or similar to the despair present in persons who have surrendered their expectations to the world of illusion created by drugs. Hope activates; despair leads to passiveness and the denial of human potential. Are you genuinely hopeful? If so, what do you hope for?

The Christian community answers those questions with a sense of confidence: "We hope for eternal life." In the letter to Titus, Paul says:

> Remind them [the members of the community of faith] . . . to be obedient, to be ready for any honest work, to speak evil of no one, to avoid

quarreling, to be gentle, and to show perfect courtesy toward all men. . . . He [God] saved us . . . in the Holy Spirit, which he poured out upon us richly through Jesus Christ our Savior, so that we might be justified by his grace and become heirs in hope of eternal life. (Titus 3 : 1–2, 5–8 RSV)

There are, of course, enormous variations in what "eternal life," "life everlasting," "immortality" or "the life to come" mean. However, Christians generally agree that for them this is the foundation of genuine hope.

2. Hope for Eternal Life

The promise of eternal life, like the biblical concept of the kingdom of God, is not simply a future notion. This hope contains confidence about what it means to be in communion with God in this life *and* in life after death. In the first instance "eternal life," as used by Paul, refers to a life that is concretely shaped by a relationship to Jesus Christ, which in turn shapes one's relationship to others. The signs of eternal life having begun now, like the kingdom which is here but not yet complete, are the evidences of a life which can be freer, more loving, and at peace. This does not mean that the Christian is never unhappy or even seriously distressed; it means that ultimately the Christian believes he or she is loved by God and God will not abandon them.

Hope for eternal life is based on the belief that Christ rose from the dead. The crucial datum, however, is not the empty tomb, but the present experience of the risen Christ in the lives of persons, and in the ongoing life of the church. The Christian hope has never depended on proof that Christ rose on the third day. Eternal life for the Christian is based on faith in the reality of Christ's resurrection. It begins now, with personal freedom from expectations of popularity, wealth, or success and with the courage to extend forgiveness and compassion to someone you dislike or who threatens you. Eternal life begins with genuine hope for the future. This means an open future where Christians can make creative and responsible decisions about vocation, family life, or community involvement, even in the face of such problems as those illustrated in the case studies. Christians believe that the Holy Spirit can touch their lives in the midst of human tragedy and joy. This is their "proof" of eternal life; it is present and powerful.

What one hopes for influences what one does, says, and feels *now*. However, eternal life also involves hope of life continuing after physical death. Paul is clear when he asks, " 'O Death, where is your victory?' " (1 Corinthians 15:55 NEB) He responds to a hard reality of life that each of us would rather avoid. A psychologist friend suggests that everyone knows that the averages on death are one out of one—for everyone except self. We each have the feeling in a crisis that we will find a way out, thus we often ignore the reality of our own death and attempt to soften the impact of the death of those we love. Particularly in America there is the tendency to ignore or avoid the harshness of dying by smothering the event with flowers, embalming fluid, or pacifying language which suggests someone has only "passed away." When Paul speaks of a Christian having "fallen asleep," this is not a denial of the reality of death, but rather an affirmation of Christ's resurrection. Paul writes, "Thanks be to God, who gives us the victory [over death] through our Lord Jesus Christ." (1 Corinthians 15:57 RSV)

Men, women, and often children do die—they are no longer physically present. Death is an unavoidable reality, and the loss of a friend or family member is a matter about which we ought to grieve. However, the Christian should "not grieve as others do who have no hope." (1 Thessalonians 4:13 RSV) Christians believe that their faith overcomes the consequences and the morbid fear of death. Most Christians do not claim to understand the exact manner of this victory over death. Thus Christians use symbols to express and dramatize their hope in Christ's victory over death. They speak of hope through the Bible, they speak in songs such as "The Saints Come Marching In" or "Swing Low, Sweet Chariot," and they speak in their creeds of the "resurrection of the dead," of "life everlasting," and, most frequently, of "eternal life."

There is a disagreement among Christians about the manner of life after death: whether it is a bodily resurrection or a spiritual resurrection. The basic issue, however, is that those who have known and experienced a relationship, a communion with God in this life, cannot believe that this communion will be destroyed by death. The God they have come to know in the Bible, in the experience of the community, and in themselves is not the sort of God who would abandon his children. The God of Christians is faithful, trustworthy, and loving.

Hope in eternal life has a concrete reality for Christians which has the power to affect how one responds now. Eternal life also has specific components of accountability and judgment. Christians believe the quality of a person's relationship with God and neighbor will ultimately be examined and evaluated. There is a difference of opinion about the matter and time of God's judgment, but most Christians have little doubt that one will be held accountable, within God's grace and mercy, for his or her individual life and the actions of the institutions and communities within which he or she lives. The promise of Christ's second coming declares that the whole world is to be judged in relationship to Christ.

Christians rely on faith because they cannot see specifically the life beyond the grave. As Paul writes, hope that is seen is not hope. Christians can hope for what they do not see because they believe that "in everything God works for good with those who love him." (Romans 8:28 RSV)

The Gift of Peace

A Christian believes that when one loves God and neighbor and hopes for eternal life, one is given a "sense of peace." Peace is, of course, not an exclusive symbol of the Christian faith any more than freedom and love. Throughout our society the symbol of peace has been prayed for, preached about, and has become one of the most important symbols of the last two decades.

Peace has a multitude of meanings. When it is used by Christians, however, it means much more than the end of armed conflict or an absence of personal and national ambition. Peace, similar to the Hebrew word *Shalom*, means wholeness, health, and security. Internal, personal peace frees men and women from dehumanization and loss of personal integrity. But peace also turns one "outward," for it supports the vision that one can truly be at peace only if others share a sense of well-being and justice. The promise and gift of peace for Christians is illustrated in a life that contains personal happiness and commitment to mutuality. You are to love your neighbor as yourself.

Christ as Prophet, Priest, and King

It would be misleading to imply in these last two chapters that the Christian view of the great themes of faith, freedom, love, hope, and peace are simply ordinary experiences in all human interaction that have been highlighted by Christianity. From the Christian perspective it would also be incorrect for one to assume that Jesus Christ is merely a great practical example or moral guide to these humanizing virtues. All these human virtues, the Christian declares, become unique in power and potential in the person and work of Jesus Christ. He was both divine and human, and seen through the Christian's spectacles of faith, his work changed the world. Chapters 2 and 3 describe Christ's work: his birth, life, death and resurrection. Chapters 4–6 describe the consequences of his work for the community of faith.

Since no Christian could fully explain this work of Christ, some believers took symbols or titles to illustrate and interpret it. This pattern of describing God's action started with images of the Old Testament, was developed in church history, and still finds a place in modern Christian celebration and ritual. Christ is called "Prophet" because he not only speaks but is the message of God, the suffering servant who gave his life for others so they may be free from bondage in life and death. Christ is called "Priest" or one who ministers to others at a point where they cannot act for themselves. In Christ's love and obedience those who believe in him are led by God to be loving and obedient. Christ as "King" reminds Christians of the claim of victory over sin and death, where hope in God's good creation is combined with the fulfillment of a new creation in Jesus Christ. By using the three offices or assignments of Prophet, Priest, and King, many Christians seek to understand and interpret Jesus' role.

Faith and freedom, love and hope, are kept alive for the Christian community by patterns of celebration. We turn to Part III for a more detailed consideration of these patterns of contemporary celebration in Christianity.

PART
III

Patterns
of Celebration

DANCE OF LIFE
Case Study D

Tears streamed down Tracy Graham's face as she blurted out her feelings to Dr. Adams. "I don't want to tell my sister that it's all right for her to die. But if I really love Sara, maybe that's what I have to say."

In talking with Dr. Adams, Sara's doctor, Tracy wanted to piece together the events of the past few months to try to understand Sara's choice to leave the hospital. Without the artificial cleansing of her blood through dialysis she could only live a few weeks. If she continued the treatment, there was a chance she could live for at least a few more years.

Tracy, now seventeen, and Sara, who would be sixteen next month, had always been very close. It was now almost six months to the day when Sara had begun to lose weight and get very weak. The family doctor said it was a kidney disease and had recommended Dr. Adams, a specialist. When both of Sara's kidneys failed, she was put on a dialysis machine which hooks up to the blood circulation system and cleans the blood of impurities as the kidneys would. Dr. Adams began to look for a donor to give Sara a healthy kidney.

Tracy remembered the arguments with her parents. She wanted to be the donor, but her mom, dad, and Sara, as well as Dr. Adams, said "no." A donor was at last found, the transplant made, but after ten days of waiting the signs were obvious that Sara's body would reject the new kidney. She was placed back on the dialysis machine. Tracy insisted again that she be the next donor. As there was a slightly better chance of her kidney being accepted, the girls' parents and Sara reluctantly agreed. Three weeks later Tracy's transplanted kidney was also rejected by Sara's body.

Tracy slipped into Sara's room. She later remembered telling Dr.

Adams how still and pale Sara had looked with all of the tubes and machines around her. There was hardly a sign of the laughing, joyous girl who had told Tracy from the time she was seven that she wanted to be a dancer. Dr. Adams had called Mr. and Mrs. Graham and Tracy into Sara's room for a conference. He told the family then that some blunt realities had to be faced. "After two rejections, we should no longer consider a kidney transplant as a possibility at this time. In a few days when Sara is stronger, she will be able to go home and resume many of her normal activities. But she must return here to the hospital three days a week for six to eight hours to use the dialysis machine. If not, her own blood would poison her.

"At the present time there is no medication that can take the place of this machine. However, there is always the hope that through new medical advances we will learn how to combat the rejection of an organ transplant." Dr. Adams had told the family in confidence yesterday that Sara might live only a short time even with dialysis because of the possibility of several complications that could arise.

The Grahams began to make plans for the future. At this point the purchase of a dialysis machine was financially an impossibility for them, and in their part of the state, none was available for rental. Thus because the family lived more than 65 miles from the hospital, Mr. Graham, who ran a small business in Oak Town, began to look for an apartment much closer to the city. Tracy knew that the medical costs for Sara had placed the family heavily in debt. The members of their village church, many of whom had been regular visitors at the hospital for the past few months, had spoken of their prayers for her, and had already held two bazaars to raise money for Sara's expenses. The money had only covered a fraction of the actual costs.

Mrs. Graham, who spent her days with Sara in the hospital, had begun to take in secretarial work in the evenings. Tracy, now in her senior year of high school, said that she really didn't want to go off to school in the fall, but would rather postpone this and get a job instead.

Sara told Tracy how aware she was of the love and support of the family and their friends. She said she was most aware of the tremendous faith they had in things working out for the best. Recently Sara had spoken to Tracy several times of their common Christian beliefs and of her assurance of a life after death. Dr. Adams had told her how lucky she was to have access to the machine. But Sara confessed to Tracy that the idea of living through the machine was very hard to take, and right now to think about life without dancing and running was almost impossible.

Sara was quite thin and took many days to recover from her second surgery. She had gotten acquainted with Mike, a boy on the same floor, and had told Tracy about him. "He's just a little guy. He's really twelve, but he looks about nine. He's waiting for a kidney donor, but unless one shows up pretty soon, he'll need the machine to make it. I even explained to him what the machine does. But I overheard two of the nurses talking. Right now there's no space available to schedule Mike for dialysis. Do you know that only one out of ten people who needs this machine gets a chance, and our hospital has one of the only machines like this in our section of the state."

That was over a week ago. Then just this morning, Sara had turned to Tracy and in a clear, firm voice said, "Trace, I can't stand the thought of living the rest of my life tied to this machine. It's not living for me. I want to go home now—and not come back to the hospital. I've already told Mom and Dad. They are very sad but I think they understand. But most important to me is that *you* understand and will support my decision."

CHAPTER 7

Rituals of Life and Death

On a rather sleepy Wednesday morning the telephone on Pastor John Phillips' desk at the church rang persistently. He was so involved in preparing the order of service for worship on Sunday, it took him a few moments to switch gears mentally and answer the phone. The woman's voice on the other end of the line asked, "John, can you please come to the house? We have just learned that our daughter was killed in a car accident." Pastor Phillips responded, "I am on my way—remember we love you."

A few seconds after John hung up the phone, it rang again. In the brief conversation that followed another member of the church, who had just learned of Carol Thompson's death, related the tragic details of the accident. Carol had just completed registration for courses to be taken during her sophomore year at the State University. She had been struck and killed as she stepped out from between two parked cars on the university campus. The automobile had been driven by another student.

As the pastor replaced the receiver and prepared to leave the office for the Thompson home, a series of thoughts flashed through his mind: Carol was an only child, adopted by Fred and Alice after unsuccessful attempts to have a child of their own. As the result of the complicated application procedures, they waited for her for several years. Carol was the joy of their life, and her growth and maturity had been celebrated with a series of events in the ritual life of the church. John Phillips had not only baptized Carol, provided instruction for her confirmation as a church member and served her first Communion, but just this summer he had also officiated at an unusually joyful wedding ceremony. At that time he had united in marriage Carol and Bill, a young man who had been her "steady" during the last two years of high school. What a devastating tragedy for her parents and Bill! Now John would be asked to conduct the last rites for Carol in a Christian funeral, attended by friends in the church and community who had shared in the events that would mark her life and death.

As Pastor Phillips fumbled for his car keys and slid behind the wheel of his car, a sudden wave of sorrow and nausea drove every thought out of his mind except one, "How can I share with Fred and Alice what God's love might mean for them in this situation—or to me, for that matter? It is a crisis like this that calls our Christian faith into question."

Arriving at the house, still filled with a good deal of anxiety, John was met at the door by Alice. As she greeted Pastor Phillips and thanked him for coming, she apologized because Fred had already left. "Left for where?" was John's surprised response. "He has gone to the campus police to find the boy who was driving the car that killed Carol," she replied. "Fred wants to tell him that it is all right. We forgive him. We don't want the boy to torture himself. God's grace will take care of him and us."

Suddenly, Pastor Phillips understood and he embraced Alice. Fred and Alice had just demonstrated one meaning of God's love. Her words, which interpreted this act of sharing and serving, had allowed John to be free and forgiving in the midst of tragedy. The event obviously had a similar effect on Alice. The pastor felt the urge to celebrate —to sing and dance and praise God, whose presence he had just unexpectedly encountered in this human drama.

The decision and action of this couple had not only helped John Phillips to understand the meaning of God's grace in a new way, but it had also "changed" him. He was certain that it had also affected the lives of Fred and Alice. Perhaps it would have the most profound influence on the life of the young driver whose name he did not even know.

This experience altered and strengthened John's relationship to Fred and Alice: eventually it would do the same for his relationship to other persons in his church and community. Finally, it significantly renewed the relationship with his God. The encounter this morning had added a new dimension to his sense of humanness.

The Role of Ritual

In thinking about Carol Thompson, John Phillips had remembered the ritual events in her church life. To shake hands, embrace, or even kiss when you meet another person; to go with friends to the movies every Saturday night; to rub your hands together and bounce the ball twice before taking a free throw in a basketball game—these are all rituals. Any practice done repeatedly or regularly in order to satisfy one's sense of fitness is a ritual act. These ritual acts have different levels of significance, but each one is a code or abbreviated meaning for an activity that is important to us. There are rituals that characterize almost every set of relationships and have a meaning that is repeatable in a shorthand form.

"Good-bye," one of the most frequently used terms in the English language, is a contraction or code for "God be with ye." This is an example not only of unrecognized religious influence on our culture, but also an example of ritual. The term developed when travel for any distance was infrequent and often dangerous. Thus it was fitting for those who stayed behind to ask God's care for the persons going on a journey. This prayer gradually became ritualized or patterned; it was contracted to "good-bye." Of course, the impact of the ritual is greater when the original intent is revived. At one time to utter "good-bye" was both a prayer and a recognition of God's power and presence in the world. Today, the ritual of "good-bye" serves a function in our language, but it does not have the same meaning as before, because most people who use it are unaware of its coded meaning.

A person's religious life is full of ritual in much the same way as one's social life. However, to those outside that religious group (and even to some within), these rituals do not have much significance if people do not understand the origin and meaning.

A religious experience was defined in the "Introduction" as a way of valuing ultimately and continually with depth and breadth. "Lived Religion" is a response to an ultimate concern; this concern influences the form of our relationships as revealed in thought and action. How does a concern shape a life, determine values, and influence personal commitments? One way this shaping comes is through a person's doing things again and again in a similar way. The regular "re-living" of words, actions, and relationships through rituals provides a pattern and meaning to our lives.

Because the rituals of the church reflect an ultimate concern, they are on a much different level of significance in the life of a believer than the everyday rituals of a handshake or a movie date. Religious rituals, however, follow the same definition: actions performed regularly which are codes for a more involved meaning.

In the life of a church member there are rituals which reveal the basic understanding that a Christian has about the relationship with God. Many of the regular activities of a Christian which reveal this understanding have been discussed as practices, such as prayer, ethics, and now worship. Worship, however, also involves many *ritual acts* which mark a significant happening in the life of a believer. These ritual acts are usually more structured and organized events than the regular practices of prayer and ethics.

These rituals, which may form "patterns of celebration," develop in every religious community to highlight crucial or pivotal events in the life of an individual believer or of the whole community of faith. For Christians these celebrations are usually linked with the remembrance, and thus "re-living," of events either in the life of Jesus or of the community which is loyal to him, the church. Because celebrations mark important transitions in a Christian's life, an anthropologist might call them "rites of passage." In the case of Carol Thompson, her birth was celebrated in baptism, her maturity in confirmation, her failures in confession or penance, her forgiveness and renewal of life in Communion or Eucharist, her union with another person in marriage, and her death in the funeral.

Worship as the Work of the People

Most ritual acts in Christianity have their focus or climax in a service of worship such as the one Pastor John Phillips was preparing when he received the call about Carol's accident. The practice of regular worship is at the very heart of the life of the Christian community. Recall that for Christians the church is not only a community of loyalty that looks to God's acts in history as the basis of their relationship with their Creator but also a community of interpretation, where beliefs and practices are constantly applied and tested against the guideline of Christ's love and freedom and a community of "symbolic action" which renews its life in the exercise of worship and through rituals. These acts of worship can be understood both as Christian practices and as Christian rituals.

Worship has at its core a notion of worth. To exercise worth-ship means to give praise to a divine being or (in the terms of this study) to one's ultimate concern. God, the source of a Christian's ultimate concern, is regarded with respect, honor, and devotion whenever Christians worship. The predominant time for conducting worship services for most Christian churches tends to be on Sunday, which is understood as the Lord's Day, or the first day of the week. This is because Christ was reputed to have been resurrected on Sunday. There are differences of opinion concerning this tradition and some Christians worship regularly on Saturday, since it coincides with the Jewish Sabbath which Jesus recognized.

It is a mistake to think that worship for all Christians is confined to formal occasions. Worship can also be understood as a conscious effort to realize the presence of God whenever and however that occurs. God is actually not more present to the worshiper than to the non-worshiper. But the worshiper can become aware of God's presence in a special way and can seek to realize that presence and thus acquire insight, not only about God, but about one's relation to the world and to one's neighbor.

In the Gospel of John Jesus stresses this attitude concerning worship in his conversation with a Samaritan woman who says, " 'Our fathers worshipped on this mountain, but you Jews say that the temple where God should be worshipped is in Jerusalem.' 'Believe me,' said Jesus, 'the time is coming when you will worship the Father neither on this mountain, nor in Jerusalem. . . . But the time approaches, indeed it is already here, when those who are real worshippers will worship the Father in spirit and in truth. Such are the worshippers whom the Father wants. God is spirit, and those who worship him must worship in spirit and in truth.' " (John 4:20–24 NEB)

Many communities of faith give a great deal of attention to occasions when the people gather for a worship service. This service is sometimes understood as a drama because various events of Christ's life and the response of his people to that life are relived. The community gathers to be created, judged, forgiven, renewed, and sent out again as a "dispersed community" of love and service. The health and wholeness of the community depends on the rhythm of a gathering and on being sent out with a fuller experience and vision of life. The Eastern Orthodox Church, along with others, speaks of this principal service as the "liturgy." The root of the word liturgy means "a work of the people." In some Christian services people become participants, not just spectators, as they respond to God's presence and promise with musical instruments, voice, or gesture as their tradition has determined is appropriate. Worship and even services of worship are virtually universal in Christianity, but no one form of this practice is in any sense universally accepted. Thus, rather than give an example of a worship service here, let us point to representative occasions in Christian worship that have a parallel pattern in most churches. We will concentrate on those rituals in the Christian community that celebrate and dramatize the relationship or encounter between a believer and his or her God. Such special events are sometimes called *sacraments,* which Augustine defined as "a visible form of an invisible grace." Most Christians believe that one or more of the sacraments are "a means of God's grace" or an "avenue toward the fullness of life."

Sacraments

1. Baptism

In a formal service of worship a mother and father present their infant child to the pastor. Standing before the entire congregation, the pastor sprinkles a few drops of water from the baptismal font on the baby's head and says, "Carol, I baptize thee in the name of the Father, and of the Son, and of the Holy Ghost." Several hundred miles away, a young woman walks into the pounding surf of the Pacific Ocean. She wears a sweat shirt declaring, "I'm a Jesus freak," and she holds the hand of the seventeen-year-old boy who is with her. She totally immerses the boy below the surging water three times and says, "You are baptized by the Spirit. Remember, Jesus is the 'one way.' " These two events are completely different in physical setting, in the method of administration, and in the words spoken. Yet both may be described as the sacrament of baptism, both use the symbol of water, and both are based on an event in Jesus' life.

A sacrament such as baptism is a "multi-media event" which uses bodily activity in a dramatic form combined with a basic symbol of everyday life. These symbols can be water, bread, wine, oil, or a ring and are considered signs of God's love and grace. Symbol is used here in a special way to refer to something, either an event, act, or object that makes what is symbolized "come alive" in one's experience. The symbol has a special relationship to that to which it points, making that event or experience really present to those in a given community who understand and employ the symbol. A sacrament is understood as "the outward and visible sign of an inward and spiritual grace given by God." Water is an absolutely essential element for life. Thus water in baptism symbolizes the belief that Jesus gives and sustains new life. Water is also a basic element for keeping clean. For this reason water also symbolizes that the person baptized has been "cleansed" of any sin by the great love of Jesus Christ.

The relationship between people is greatly influenced by symbols. For example, a kiss may be a symbol of love. The kiss points to the reality of love which stands behind it. The kiss expresses the love it symbolizes. Of course, symbols like kisses can be misused to mislead and manipulate others. Even in the New Testament scriptures, Judas, one of Jesus' disciples, betrayed him to the authorities with a kiss. However, when the symbol is genuinely employed, it has the power to re-create the feeling or event, and thus to concentrate or code the meaning of the experience it symbolizes.

Those Christians who recognize baptism—which includes members of all the larger churches except Quaker and the Salvation Army—understand it to be such a symbolic ritual event. They believe that baptism reflects the capacity of human beings to perceive and receive God's love. Baptism is based on Mark 1:9 which says, "Jesus came from Nazareth of Galilee and was baptized by John in the Jordan." (RSV) Christians usually consider it as the sacrament of initiation into the Christian Church. Baptism is linked with a person's birth, with his or her being "born again" into the Christian faith. In infant baptism the child is called by her Christian name, e.g., "Carol," and given that name "In the name of the Trinity," to remind Christians of her new birth.

The symbolism of being totally immersed in the water, which is insisted on by Baptists and others, reflects one view of Jesus' baptism (Mark 1:10). Paul also speaks of this meaning of baptism in his letter to the Church in Rome:

> Do you not know that all of us who have been baptized into Christ Jesus were baptized into his death? We were buried therefore with him by baptism into death, so that as Christ was raised from the dead by the glory of the Father, we too might walk in newness of life.
>
> For if we have been united with him in a death like his, we shall certainly be united with him in a resurrection like his. (Romans 6:3–5 RSV)

For those Christians who follow this understanding total immersion symbolizes dying to an old life, being buried, and rising again with Christ.

Another symbolic activity in the ritual of baptism is that of washing, which highlights the reason for using water. The minister or priest usually asks questions concerning the belief and commitment of the individual if he or she is an adult, or of the parents in the case of infant baptism. The answers involve a profession of faith in Jesus as Lord. From the third century A.D. the Apostles' Creed was often used as a baptismal profession of belief. The "washing away" of previous sins, and the forgiveness of all that one has been, is enacted in the immersing or in the pouring on of water. So the candidate emerges out of the water into a new and fuller life having been "baptized into Jesus Christ." Some people were baptized in the nude in the early church; they laid aside their old garments that represented their former life and received, after their baptism, a new white robe. Many infants still wear long white baptismal dresses for their baptism. Historically, this robe was a way to dramatize visually the newness of life and the innocence or forgiveness of sins which results from "putting on Jesus Christ."

This rite of initiation, since it represents new birth, may be performed in most Christian churches only once. As Luther remarked, however, the faith which was confessed at baptism (either by the new Christian or by the parents) should be nourished and strengthened until death. Thus the baptismal basin or font is located at the entrance to the church or in the front of the sanctuary and is used at each new baptism to remind Christians that they have been accepted by God and remain in his love. Baptism is the sacrament of life and death that makes it possible to identify with Jesus and the church in the quest for fullness of life.

2. Confirmation

Continuing to compare Christian patterns of celebration to the most important stages of human life and death, a Christian, in those denominations in which there is infant baptism, proceeds from baptism to confirmation. Confirmation is for many Christians just what the name implies—the confirmation of the promises or covenants made by a Christian or made on his behalf at baptism. Confirmation is the "rite of passage" into greater spiritual responsibility or maturity in the Christian community. This ritual has its parallel in the Jewish Bar Mitzvah and even in the adolescent circumcision rites of some African Traditional Religions.

What event in your life, if any, signaled to the world, in an official and dramatic way, your new maturity and responsibility within a particular group. How was your full membership in that society recognized? This is the role of a "rite of passage," which some have argued is needed in our society, generally, to establish both the responsibilities of and limits on young people. Some Christian churches recognize confirmation as the sacrament of initiation which announces new responsibilities.

It is probably evident in this last qualification, "some Christian churches," that not all Christians accept confirmation as a sacrament. In fact a genuine difference of opinion exists in the church as to how many sacraments there are. Roman Catholic, Eastern Orthodox, and some Episcopalians count seven: Baptism, Confirmation, Communion, Marriage, Unction (the rite connected with the anointing of the sick and dying), Penance (private confession and forgiveness of sins), and Holy Orders (ordination to the ministry). A majority of Protestants would accept only baptism and Communion as sacraments directly established by Jesus Christ. A minority of Christians reject all sacraments. Despite the significant debates over the number, form, and meaning of the sacraments (which have even contributed to division in the church), most Christians celebrate in some way the events in the life of a believer which the sacraments commemorate.

In many churches confirmation may be understood as a ritual in which the grace of the Holy Spirit is sent in a new or fuller way to those who have already received the Spirit in some way at baptism. Confirmation is based on an account in scripture where the Apostles Peter and John were sent to those people in Samaria who had heard about Jesus. Peter and John prayed for them and "then they laid their hands on them and they received the Holy Spirit." (Acts 8:17 RSV) In the Christian church today children are confirmed at some time between the ages of seven and sixteen. The ritual is preceded by instruction concerning the tradition and wisdom of the Christian faith, as initiation rites have done throughout human history. For Roman Catholics and Episcopalians, the sacrament is administered by a bishop. For most Protestants confirmation occurs in the local congregation, administered by the pastor; it follows instruction, public examination of beliefs, and a statement of one's faith. This was the form of confirmation for Carol Thompson. In some churches, including the Orthodox, a person is confirmed immediately after baptism. This "relives" an event in Christ's life. The writer of the Gospel of John reports that immediately following Jesus' Baptism, "'I saw the Spirit descend as a dove from heaven, and it remained on him.'" (John 1:32 RSV) There are groups of Christians in several churches who call themselves "charismatics." For them baptism by the Holy Spirit is a special event that often brings the power to speak in tongues, called glossolalia, and to heal. These believers trace this special gift back to the gathering of the disciples at Pentecost following Jesus' resurrection (see Chapter 3). As this event is recorded in Acts, ". . . they were all filled with the Holy Spirit and began to speak in other tongues, as the Spirit gave them utterance." (Acts 2:4 RSV) In most churches, though the pattern of the ritual varies, confirmation tends to confirm God's gift of full life through the activity of the Holy Spirit. Also in most churches this gift of the Spirit in confirmation is preparation for taking Communion or the Eucharist.

3. Confession

There are only two of all the sacraments in the Christian church that not only may, but must be repeated: Repentance (confession) and the Eucharist. Repentance is a necessary preparation or prerequisite for the Eucharist (Communion) in some Christian traditions. In this action the Christian confesses his or her sins and is granted forgiveness or absolution (a "setting free" of guilt or obligation). For Roman Catholics this also often involves the acceptance of penalties such as additional daily prayers. They call the sacrament Penance. Repentance by Christians is a form of prayer and was discussed in Chapter 5 as a Christian practice. However, in many churches a confession of sin is also understood as a ritual and a more structured response than spontaneous prayer. Confession may be said privately or corporately, that is, when the whole congregation prays together.

Remember that Christians believe that Jesus not only healed, but he also forgave sins. When a paralysed man lying on a bed was brought to him, Jesus said, " 'Take heart, my son; your sins are forgiven.' " Some of the lawyers present criticized Jesus for being presumptuous enough to think he could forgive sins, something only God could do. So Jesus said to the lawyers, " 'Is it easier to say, "your sins are forgiven," or to say, "Stand up and walk"? But to convince you that the Son of Man [a title attributed to Jesus] has the right on earth to forgive sins,'—he turned to the paralysed man—'Stand up, take your bed, and go home.' Thereupon the man got up, and went off home." (Matthew 9:2–7 NEB)

In the Lord's Prayer Christians pray, "Forgive us our debts [sins or trespasses] as we forgive our debtors [those who have sinned/trespassed against us]." The symbol of kneeling expresses the Christian's sorrow and desire for forgiveness. Most Roman Catholics confess individually and privately to a priest; many Protestants include a prayer of confession as a regular part of the worship service, and other groups like the Salvation Army confess their sins publicly in a spiritual meeting. Whichever form is taken, and whether it is considered a sacrament, as it is for Roman Catholics and the Orthodox, or a significant ritual of worship, penance involves first a confession. This confession must include genuine sorrow for one's sin and failures and the intention not to repeat them if possible. Confession is followed by forgiveness or absolution of guilt. This may include a sign of the Christian's repentance such as the saying of extra prayers or giving service. It could involve the public pronouncement of forgiveness in the name of Jesus Christ. The change in a Christian's life brought about by confession is the commitment to forgive others for their failures—even as God in Jesus Christ has forgiven them. For the Christian, sins are a barrier between a Christian and God, until they are confessed. Then they become a bridge to Christ's forgiving love. It is then, with a fuller awareness of Christ's love, that a Christian feels he or she can come to Communion.

4. The Lord's Supper

Holy Communion, Mass, Holy Eucharist (which means in Greek "to give thanks") is the one sacrament around which all the other rituals revolve, since it seeks to incorporate the central themes of Jesus' life and ministry. This ritual seeks to enact Jesus' last meal with his disciples. For this reason it is also called "The Lord's Supper." The bread and wine of the meal symbolize that Christ remains "in communion" and thus present with those who believe in him.

The disciples were sharing a meal which recalled the Jewish feast of the Passover. This feast commemorates the Exodus when God liberated the Israelites from the oppression of the Egyptians and made his covenant with them. At the supper Jesus took the bread and wine, gave thanks to God, and offered it to his disciples saying of the bread which he had just broken, "'Take this and eat; this is my body.'" Then Jesus held the cup of wine and offered it with these words, "'Drink from it, all of you. For this is my blood, the blood of the covenant, shed for many for the forgiveness of sins.'" (Matthew 26:26–28 NEB) In his letter to the Corinthians, Paul passed on essentially the same tradition of the supper (1 Corinthians 11:23–26), except Paul added that Jesus instructs his disciples to continue the ritual as a memorial. Paul reminds the church, "For every time you eat this bread and drink the cup, you proclaim the death of the Lord, until he comes." (1 Corinthians 11:26 NEB)

Some Christians emphasize that the Communion ritual is a memorial of Christ's sacrifice. Those in the Roman Catholic and Orthodox tradition generally believe that when the priest blesses or consecrates the bread and wine, these elements are changed ("transubstantiated") and become Christ's actual body and blood. Most Protestants believe that the body and blood are represented only spiritually; others regard the Communion simply as a memorial act. Whichever understanding is held, there is a core belief that in the event of sharing the bread and the wine in Christ's name, there is a reality to his presence and power. The believer can relive the experience of Christ's death and resurrection and thus refresh the promise of eternal life. John Calvin caught this spirit of real presence and the difficulty of explanation when he declared that to "feed on Christ" is a secret "too lofty for either my mind to comprehend or my words declare.... I rather experience than understand."

Not only does Communion express Christ's presence and sacrifice, it also includes a promise of forgiveness, the consummation of confession, which involves a renewal or fresh beginning to life. There is a special sense of fellowship experienced by those who share this sacrament that spans distance, language, and culture. It draws people together as members of Christ's body, the church. This was true in the case of Ted Lee while he worshiped and took Communion in the Fiji Islands. The Lord's Supper is the sacrament of unity in Christ, both of those present at the service and of Christians around the earth. This unity is symbolized in such annual celebrations as Worldwide Communion Sunday, a selected date following Easter on which thousands of Christians around the world share the Eucharist in their own congregations.

Ironically, the very event that proclaims unity in Christ is the occasion that divides Christians from each other in worship because of differences of opinion about the form of the sacrament or who is eligible to share at Christ's table. It is precisely because the sacrament has such immense significance that Christians are anxious to guard it by declaring who, when, and how this sacrament may be celebrated. It is the importance of this re-creation which often makes the event so solemn and serious. This tone stresses the link with Christ's death by crucifixion on Good Friday. Equally important is the thankful and joyful praise that ties the Communion to Christ's resurrection on Easter morning.

5. Marriage and Ordination

There are two ritual events which are not in the pattern of every Christian's life as are the other sacraments. These two occasions of worship celebrate a special calling and special responsibilities. Carol Thompson had participated in one with her husband Bill—marriage. Pastor Phillips had experienced the other in his preparation for ministry in Christ's church—ordination. Both activities include symbols of union with God and other persons, and promises or vows that are made before God and representatives of the community. Marriage and Ordination, sacraments for Catholics, Orthodox, and many Episcopalians, are celebrations of the "rite of passage" from one status to another, and from one set of responsibilities to new ones.

Have you wondered why there is often an exchange of rings during a wedding ceremony? The ring is a symbol and pledge of the couples' covenant of love and responsibility. The scriptures use a most dramatic image of both the union and the eternity of this relationship (represented in the unbroken circle of the ring), when they declare, "*the two will become one body.*" (Ephesians 5:31 JB)

Christians understand marriage as instituted by God in the creation story and "sanctified" or made sacred by Jesus in his presence at a marriage service in Cana when, for the sake of the celebration of this union, he is reported to have turned water into wine. For Christians the union is not only between two people. It is also before God and one's brothers and sisters in Christ who, by attendance at the marriage service, signify their promise to support this union. Did you realize what your attendance at a Christian wedding implies? Perhaps invitations should not be so casually accepted!

Paul employs the most intimate image for marriage when he says, "...even as Christ also loved the church, and gave himself for it.... So ought men to love their wives as their own bodies.... This is a great mystery: but I speak concerning Christ and the church." (Ephesians 5:25, 28, 32 KJV) Christian marriage gives special recognition to human love and the status of family life, including the procreation and education of children. Since the church sees itself as blessing the promises (vows) of love and responsibility made in the ritual of marriage, many pastors and priests offer pre- and post-marital counseling, interpret the church's guidelines that govern divorce and remarriage, and enable church support for the education of children. Marriage celebrates the calling to love and life.

The response of the call of God through the church to the ordained ministry involves a smaller number of men and women. Have you ever witnessed in person or on TV the ordination (to "establish by order") of a minister, pastor, priest, elder, deacon, or bishop (titles depending on the denomination) and seen the ritual of persons gathering around to lay their hands on the head of the candidate for ordination? This symbol of union of the person with God and all those who serve the church is a ritual act of passing on the covenant of responsibility involved in the Christian ministry. This act is based on Christ's words to his disciples when he appeared to them after his resurrection: " 'Peace be with you. As the Father has sent me, even so I send you.' " (John 20:21 RSV) We learn in the book of Acts that disciples of the early church decided to appoint " 'seven men of good repute, full of the Spirit and of wisdom' " to serve the people and "laid their hands upon them" to confirm their choice (Acts 6:3, 6 RSV).

The ritual of ordination recognizes the calling or setting aside of a man or woman for special forms of ministry. One is called by God through the action of the church. Ordination requires special forms of preparation or training that differ according to the office or position to which one is ordained. The conditions for ordination are specified by each branch of the church. In some traditions ordination to the priesthood requires that one be unmarried or celibate so that one's total attention can be devoted to ministry. Many churches also ordain lay persons to offices in the church such as elder or deacon. Whether officially ordained to an office and a function, many Christians believe that each by virtue of his or her baptism and confession of Christ is summoned to share and to serve out of love of God and neighbor.

6. The Funeral

The patterns of celebration in Christianity seek to integrate the basic elements of life in the drama of ritual. The most important moments in the life of a believer and of his or her community are celebrated by being lifted up in worship and linked with the life of Jesus Christ. How then, by comparison to the other joyous rituals cited in this chapter, can Christians speak of a funeral as a celebration of life?

To "celebrate" a death does not necessarily mean a joyous occasion, although it can mean that in some communities, even in reference to a Christian funeral. More than that, celebration means to proclaim or dramatize an event. We make the event "famous" by turning it into a play so that the participants in the drama can see that this involves more than the death of Carol or perhaps Sara Graham; for the Christian the funeral also involves the death of Jesus Christ. The primary significance of a Christian funeral, however, is that it relates not only to Christ's death but also to his resurrection and his ultimate victory over death. The Christian ritual of the funeral service proclaims in a dramatic way that a community shares the belief of Sara Graham that physical death is not the final end of life.

The Christian believes that somehow Carol and Sara shall not be separated from the love of God, their good creator. By Christ's death and resurrection Christians believe they will be present with him in an eternal life which is even fuller than the life they have known here. The details of that eternal life are a mystery for most Christians; it is the promise and hope that are realities. For these reasons the Christian funeral becomes the celebration not of death alone but of the eternal life that it ushers in.

In some Christian churches, such as the Roman Catholic and Orthodox, there is also a sacred act or sacrament performed either at the time of illness or approaching death that gives the reassurance of the salvation and wholeness promised in eternal life. In the Orthodox tradition the symbol of oil rubbed on the body in Unction (the act of anointing) is understood to represent the healing "oil of prayer." Christians believe they can celebrate either physical or spiritual healing in the reliving of Christ's death and resurrection. This happens as they proclaim eternal life in the death and promised resurrection of a Carol or a Sara.

Sara's Ritual of Death and Life

Have you been wondering how the case of the "Dance of Life" turned out? Previously the authors have resisted telling you the outcome of these actual cases for fear it might suggest there is a "right" answer. We genuinely believe that either decision by Sara, made with her family and her friends, could have been responsible and loving according to the values of her Christian faith.

There is a very strong case for Sara, as a Christian, to have continued to hope that she would get well. Many people in the church had prayed for this to happen, and Dr. Adams said there was always a chance that new drugs and techniques would be discovered. Sara considered her life to be a gift of God; therefore she might have reasoned that it was not up to her or her parents to "give back" that life. The decision to continue to live with God's help and to continue to witness to God's love, even in the midst of her tragedy, would have been a responsible decision from the Christian perspective. However, Sara decided to go home and die. She made this decision for the sake of the quality of her own life and for that of other patients like Mike, because of her belief in the promise of eternal life, because of a deep love for her family, and finally for the sake of her own freedom to die with dignity. All of these sources informed her decision.

Some of the medical doctors had difficulty believing that Sara really understood the consequences of her decision. They feared that Sara was under such pressure and strain from the pain and confinement of the past months that the family would make a fatal error by complying with Sara's wishes. So the doctors insisted that the Grahams take a series of psychological tests to indicate their mental competence at this moment. Sara and her parents took the tests and passed them. Sara made the last months of her life a testimony to the strength of her own Christian conviction and commitment. She shared and served in her relationship to Tracy, her parents, and members of the church and community. Friends later said they had found in Sara a commitment to God's gift of the fullness of life that they had seldom seen so dramatically but quietly revealed. Therefore, the decision to sacrifice her present existence for the fullness of life in others, her own family and Mike, caused her actions to proclaim and celebrate the power of her Christian faith.

Following Sara's death two months after leaving the hospital, the service of worship called a funeral became a celebration of eternal life. There was genuine and natural sorrow and grief over the loss of Sara's physical presence from the community. But there was no sorrow for Sara on the part of those who understood the meaning of this ritual. There was genuine joy for Sara and for a community called the church that had experienced a proclamation of eternal life and a witness to its reality and its power. This worship service was a ritual of death and life.

Lord of the Dance

Significant events in a Christian's life are given new meaning as they are seen in unison with the power and events of Jesus Christ's life. A Christian's baptism, confirmation, confession, communion, death and resurrection, and perhaps a marriage or ordination have their value and significance expressed in the worship of the community. Christians believe that the pageantry and power of even a simple worship service can declare Christ's love in words and symbolic acts. The Christian seeks to declare in gestures and in the praise of music and song that God is present. "God with us" is the shorthand ritual essence of Christian worship.

Perhaps the Christian understanding of God's power and presence can best be conveyed through a contemporary Christian song that speaks particularly to the reality of the human situation for both the Thompson and the Graham families. This song weaves together Carol's and Sara's lives as believers and the life of Jesus Christ as the "Lord of the Dance."

I DANCED IN THE MORNING
(Lord of the Dance)

Sydney Carter, 1963   Based on a Shaker tune
Arr. and adapted by Sydney Carter, 1963

1.

I danced in the morning when the world was begun,
And I danced in the moon and the stars and the sun
And I came down from heaven and I danced on the earth—
At Bethlehem I had my birth.

Refrain:
Dance, then, wherever you may be,
I am the Lord of the Dance, said he,
And I'll lead you all, wherever you may be,
And I'll lead you all in the dance, said he.

2.

I danced for the scribe and the Pharisee,
But they would not dance and they wouldn't follow me;
I danced for the fishermen, for James and John—
They came with me and the dance went on.

3.

I danced on the Sabbath and I cured the lame;
The holy people said it was a shame;
They whipped and they stripped and they hung me high,
And they left me there on a cross to die.

4.

I danced on a Friday and the sky turned black.
It's hard to dance with the devil on your back;
They buried my body and they thought I'd gone.
But I am the dance and I still go on.

5.

They cut me down and I leap up high—
I am the life that'll never, never die;
I'll live in you if you'll live in me—
I am the Lord of the Dance, said he.

CHAPTER 8

The Core of Christianity

In the midst of a spring nighttime storm, the lightning flashed across the sky and thunder cracked so loudly it made the china shiver and the dog howl. The scene was an old city brownstone three stories high, at about one o'clock in the morning. It suddenly dawned on Bill Hopkins that the three children sleeping on the third floor might be frightened by the storm. He went bounding up the stairs to comfort them. He discovered that the children were already huddled together in the bottom of one bunk bed.

As Bill entered the room, the lightening flashed again and illuminated the rain which was coming down in sheets against the windows of the third floor. As he sat down on the side of the bed, he looked out at the spectacle and said to his children in an enthusiastic voice, "Look what a magnificent show God is putting on for us! I can feel God's presence and power right here in the room." Jane, his four-year-old, looked up and said, "If you want to stay up here with God, it's all all right with me. But I'm going down and sleep with Mama where it's safe."

The commitment to and application of one's religious belief is a risky business. It is difficult to act confidently and consistently on the basis of an ultimate concern. The Christian faith puts its believers in a "bind" by insisting that they are responsible for their neighbors—even those they don't like. The Christian is constantly forced to ask, "Is this the loving and responsible thing to do?" At one time or another most Christians feel like Jane when they are faced with such a demand to share and serve: they would rather sleep with mother where it's safe.

When one must decide about birth or abortion, service with sacrifice, freedom in limits, death and eternal life, as well as the more immediate daily choices, the resources of Christianity may provide some assistance. The eyeglasses of Christian faith serve as *one* perspective that may clarify the situation or give some guidelines for a responsible decision that will reflect your values and commitments. This study has sought to acquaint you with those resources, to urge you to try on the glasses through which millions of persons see the world. The purpose has not been to persuade you to order a similar set of lenses, but rather to appreciate and evaluate how others who consider themselves Christians see the world. This text has sought to illustrate that the Christian perspective is *one viable option* for understanding the reality of human life in the world.

The view of one's world, particularly when it is being slashed by a storm or a special crisis, will be different for each person. Some, like the father in our story, will perceive the world as a place that gives evidence of God's power and presence. Life may often be threatening, but it is basically a good creation in which God takes a personal interest. Others will interpret the world from a different perspective and thus draw different conclusions about how one should react to the storm. In either case one's responses will involve value judgments of relative or ultimate concern. The task of this study has been to encourage the reader to be more sensitive to what one's statements and actions say about who one is and what he or she considers important.

Worldwide Celebrations

On the Thursday preceding Easter Sunday in Rome the head of the most populous church in Christendom lays aside his gold encrusted robes and the sceptre which is a symbol of his office as Pope. He then takes up a basin of water and a towel. As the organ plays, he stoops to wash the feet of persons present at the Maundy Thursday service. He does this in response to Christ's command ("Maundy"), " 'Then if I, your Lord and Master, have washed your feet, you also ought to wash one another's feet. I have set you an example: you are to do as I have done for you.' " (John 13:14-15 NEB) This pattern of celebration in Rome symbolizes Jesus' commands of service and humility.

On Good Friday not far from Nairobi, Kenya in East Africa a group of Christians gathers together on the edge of the bush. They nail one of their members, who has volunteered for this role, onto the tall stump of a living tree made into a cross by the addition of another branch. Though this man does not actually die, Christians, accompanied by the beat of the drum and rhythm of the gourd rattle, remember and mourn the suffering and agony of their Lord Jesus Christ on this darkest day in the Christian year. They also mourn for the suffering and agony in their part of the "developing world" as their brothers and sisters seek the liberation that Christ promises to all men and women. Later in the year that same tree stump sprouts a new branch, understood by these believers as a symbol of life rising out of Christ's death on Good Friday.

On the Saturday before Easter the streets of Seville are crammed with thousands of people watching a procession which has a remarkable combination of robed and hooded figures. Some, rejoicing in the events of Easter week, hand out candy to crowds of children. Others are barefoot penitents carrying heavy wooden crosses as they slowly walk through the streets. Eighty other members of the procession bear the enormous image of the Madonna of the Diamond Tear on a great litter. The men are carrying this *pasos* through the long parade route to the central cathedral for blessing. Sorrow and joy are combined in the symbols of humiliation and triumph during Holy Week in southern Spain.

As midnight on the eve of Easter Sunday approaches, a large congregation waits outside the doors of the Greek Orthodox cathedral in Athens. The rich vestments of the priests shine, incense fills the air, and the excitement of the people who join the crowd grows as they symbolically seek for the body of Jesus in the tomb. The bishop knocks three times on the huge cathedral doors. Suddenly the doors are flung open and the cry goes up, "Christ is risen!" The congregation presses into the church to participate in the divine service (liturgy), which is followed by a great feast celebrating Christ's resurrection.

On Sunday morning near the shore on the northern end of Viti

Levu, the largest of the Fiji Islands, a group of Christians are drawn by the beat of a great lali drum. They greet the sunrise with the special joy of Easter morning. The frying of fish on the beach reminds them of the original disciples of Christ, the fishermen who also waited for his resurrection. This morning they are joined by several Indian Christians whose countrymen now compose half of the Fijian population. In the nineteenth century British colonial policy imported thousands of laborers from India to work in the sugar cane fields. Tension and even occasional violence has characterized the relationship between Fijians and Indians. On this morning, however, they come together to celebrate the great symbol of reconciliation. Jesus' resurrection binds Christians together as brothers and sisters in Christ.

The last four days of Holy Week, the week preceding Easter, are the climax of the Christian year. The patterns of celebration of these days relive events in Christ's life. Each of the celebrations, however, takes a different form, depending on the culture and tradition of the community that remembers these events. The events and celebrations of Holy Week illustrated above are not necessarily representative of Christian practice in these cultures, but they contain characteristic features of the expression of Christian faith. The Christian perspective has been spread throughout the world by Christians who sought to share the good news of the gospel. Evangelism, a name for this process, means bearing a message of good news about God's renewing of all humankind in Jesus Christ. This kind of mission takes many forms: the construction of a hospital in Brazil; a Billy Graham revival in Madison Square Garden, New York; a "self-development of peoples" project for training industrial workers in Hong Kong; or a simple sharing by one friend to another of what Christian faith says about business ethics. All of these are ways that Christians share and serve from their own Christian perspective.

It must be acknowledged that some approaches in the history of mission violated the Christian theme of liberation by suppressing and even oppressing the human worth and distinctive culture of the peoples with whom the faith was shared. For example, in the early stages of Christian mission to Africa, missionaries often insisted that local people abandon traditional rituals, cultural patterns, and even forms of music and dance. The villagers were then told they had to adopt Western styles of dress, education, and even language if they wished to accept the Christian faith. The persistent style of Christian witness, however, is for each culture to discover and express its own understanding of Christianity in indigenous or local ways. Thus the music, dress, language, ceremonies, art, even thought forms of Christianity are expressive of distinctive ways of seeing and interpreting the world through the eyeglasses of the Christian faith. It is this continued indigenization (localization) of theological expression which some Christian leaders believe is a major task of the church in the years just ahead.

The tree of Christianity, to return to our original image, has its roots nurtured in many different soils. These varied cultural soils contribute to the richness and diversity of the plant. One might respond then that the message of Christianity cannot remain strong if there are so many different patterns of celebration and ways of understanding the message. The fear of fragmentation and division can be very real. A story that illustrates this concern took place several years ago in the center of a large midwestern university. One of the fraternity houses was having a terrible time keeping available parking spaces for their members in the house lot. Announcements and threats of all kinds had little result in curbing the illegal parking of dozens of cars. Finally, one member of the house came up with an idea that might solve the problem. He placed a sign at the entrance to the parking lot which read: ALL CARS PARKED HERE ILLEGALLY WILL BE DISASSEMBLED. The sign was effective! The fear of having their cars taken apart was strong enough to make drivers look for other places to park. The fear of being disassembled, either physically or figuratively, is also a legitimate concern of any religious community. However, the benefits of diversity may well outweigh the fear of disunity.

How does one rejoice in the richness of diversity? Is it possible to celebrate religious pluralism in which each group takes into account the interests and values of its own expression of commitment and faith? It seems to the authors' imperative, in the midst of a world that contains many religions other than Christianity which command respect, as well as an enormous variety of interpretations and expressions of Christian history, practice, and belief, that no one religious group claims to possess a monopoly on spiritual values and insight. We need more than tolerance of other perspectives on the reality of human life in the world. What seems required is an *appreciative* but *critical respect* for religious traditions which differ from one's own. The goal is to seek not accomodation, but cooperation in those areas that influence the quality of human life. Persons and communities of this world have become so interdependent that any other course would endanger the more fully human style of life we all seek.

The flowering of radically different forms of celebration in Christianity should not necessarily be seen as a threat to the health of the total tree of Christianity. The variety of forms of worship do not change the central Christian message of God's love any more than the different ways people perceive a tree alter the tree itself. The authors have maintained that there is a core to this tree of Christianity, which when recognized and constantly updated and reinterpreted, may keep Christians in creative conversation with one another and with other fellow human beings who seek to be free, responsible, and fulfilled.

The Core of Christianity

This study has presented one picture of the core of Christianity. The sketch will and should be challenged by others who would see it in different ways. We trust, however, that both this picture and that of others will be recognizable as drawings of the same tree and that a comparison of these understandings will assist in creating the reader's representation.

Let us now review our picture of Christianity as an art critic might. He or she might ask what themes were reflected in the painting. Three viewpoints informed the artists' preparation.

Setting and Historical Development
Basic Beliefs and Practices
Patterns of Celebration.

Three basic colors blend throughout the work and are exposed from different angles like the growth rings on a tree which are apparent no matter where you slice into the trunk. The basic Christian commitments are:

Faith in God's good creation
    Love of God and neighbor
        Hope in eternal life.

Three fundamental motifs bring the painting alive in an attempt to depict the original scene in all its richness and vitality. The central rituals that dramatize the Christian life are:

Baptism as birth through faith in God the Father
    Communion as death and resurrection with Christ the Son
        Celebration of eternal life as a gift of the Holy Spirit.

Ultimately the value of the painting will depend on your response to it. A friend who is an artist staunchly refuses to say what her paintings "mean." She says that the impact of a work of art should result from each person's encounter with it. It is with this understanding of art that the authors see their particular presentation of Christianity. We would hope our drawing might make the story of Christianity more intelligible and accessible to Christians and non-Christians alike as they analyze, seek to understand, and are critical of the history, beliefs, and rituals of Christianity.

PART
IV

Resource Guide for Teachers and Learners

INTRODUCTION

A colleague from Harvard University confesses that he is a "learcher" (resulting from a combination of lear-ner and tea-cher and pronounced "lurcher"). This is the often uncomfortable combination of a person who seeks to be a co-learner with his or her students while at the same time carrying the responsibility for a significant role as teacher. To be a skilled facilitator of the learning process is always an art that must be constantly nurtured, but it is especially difficult in the area of religion which is concerned with valuing and how that affects one's life. Christianity, like Judiasm, is a particularly sensitive area because many persons understand their own values to have been influenced by one or both of these two dominant religious traditions of the Western world.

Since religion plays such an important role in the lives of many people, the would be "learcher" of a religion has a special responsibility to see that the conscience and commitments of each learner are respected and appreciated. It is also crucial that the teacher strive to create an atmosphere of free and open inquiry in which persons may extend knowledge by engagement as co-learners with the teacher.

Purpose of the Guide

The goal of this Guide is to help you "learch" along more easily as you enjoy this book on Christianity. The suggestions seek to enhance one's role as a facilitator of the learning process and offer ways in which the material may be handled in a relevant and an exciting way for both teachers and students, discussion leaders, and participants.

Ideas in the Guide emerged from case studies, projects, films, etc. that have been field tested in high school classrooms and church schools across a broad spectrum of the socio-economic scale. Obviously some material works better in one setting than another. The spark that makes for a good class experience depends on the selection and implementation of some of the ideas suggested here and on others developed through a leader's own experience. Throughout the Guide, the authors have tried to avoid advocating any one particular approach or teaching strategy. The emphasis will be on flexibility, availability, and clarity.

Contents of the Guide

1. An introduction to the case-study approach is integral to the experiential dimension of this study of Christianity. There are also separate teaching suggestions for each one of the four case studies included in the volume.
2. Each chapter in the text is dealt with separately and according to the same pattern. The variety of options open to the teacher are listed as:
   (a) Suggested Study Questions. These focus on the core issues of each chapter and seek to encourage the student to consolidate and apply his or her learnings.
   (b) Suggested Projects and Activities. The majority of these are designed for small groups or individuals who wish to do further research on a particular topic.
   (c) Audio-Visual Materials. Though each item is described to aid you in choice and ordering, the authors assume any film will be previewed prior to classroom use.
   (d) Bibliography. This section contains a selected and annotated list of additional references for each chapter.
3. An annotated general bibliography suggests basic resources for the entire volume.

Teaching With Cases

A case study is a *true* story that does not have a conclusion or an "answer." The account of a life situation such as Sue Ann and Danny's decision about having an abortion, or Peter and Jane Murphy's decision about joining the Peace Corps, does not, in the opinion of the authors, have a "right" answer. However, some responses are better than others. The excitement and power of cases as a learning tool is to allow participants to discover for themselves not only what decision the person in the case should make, but what decision *they* would make in a similar situation and *why*. Through extensive field testing, the authors have found that these actual cases about high school and college students and their families provide a provocative link between the content of the text and the actual situation of learners. The authors see the task of the learner as coming to a basic understanding of Christianity, being able to evaluate it critically, and interpreting it for her or himself and others; the cases provide an interesting and engaging way to accomplish this aim.

The analogy between a case and a mystery is suggested in the "Introduction." A mystery has clues to be discovered and put together in order to reach a viable solution, as determined by the students' values. The case teacher in this situation is not the traditional dispenser of knowledge. Rather, he or she is a co-learner along with the students in analyzing the clues and proposing responsible and creative solutions. The main function of the case discussion leader is to foster a meaningful dialogue between the participants, to highlight verbally or on the blackboard the issues and insights they discover, and finally, to assist in the summary of the participants' insights as a consequence of discussing the case.

The case-study approach has the potential for extensive participation and a high level of interest and involvement on the part of the class. As one teacher said to the authors after using the method, "Two students shared today who have not spoken in three months. It was a miracle!" The miracle depends, we think, on the fact that the cases are genuinely self-involving. A learner gets gradually drawn into the story and then wants to share a question or insight. However, most learners only want to share if the style of the case teachers is supportive and affirming. Participants discover quickly in this approach if the teacher has a hidden agenda (namely, where the teacher thinks the case should come out), or if their ideas are not taken seriously.

As case teachers, we seek to convey our affirmation of a participant's personhood by attempting to record on the blackboard the essence of what a speaker has contributed to the conversation. Sometimes we may ask him or her to clarify what was said or even rephrase it, and then ask, "Is this what you are getting at . . . ?" Sharing our real questions and insights occurs most frequently in the supportive atmosphere that allows for intellectual and personal risk, and often growth. Most discussion leaders are very sensitive about listening. However, the case method can be unusually effective in drawing out personal responses and the case teacher must be extremely sensitive to participants' comments.

Teacher Preparation

One particularly challenging part of the case teacher's role is to guide the discussion in fruitful paths, assuming responsibility for the direction of discussion without determining the outcome of the dialogue. Consequently, preparation of a case is very important. The authors suggest that the teacher read each case carefully, perhaps listing: the central issues; the principal characters and their feelings; the major events and dates in the case; and finally, the possible alternatives that might be proposed. The case teacher should think through the various paths the case might take—not to supply an answer, but to enable better learning in the form of clear questions or data. A suggested teaching note in the form of a series of questions has been included in the Guide for each case. This is only an aid to a discussion leader's own creative imagination based on classroom experience with each case. At the end of a case discussion many leaders also add to their teaching notes new ideas suggested by participants.

How to Begin

A case teacher may want to begin the first case, not by assigning it the day before, but by asking everyone to turn to "A Matter of Life and Death" at the beginning of the discussion and to read it through. The authors often encourage participants to read it a second time, if they finish early, and to look for the important problems in the case. This technique takes pressure off slower readers so that everyone will take the time to read the case carefully and all start from the same base. This may take about five minutes. The class might then begin with the question, "What is the situation in the case? What does the problem seem to be?" Questions like these tend to get the dialogue started; the second step will be in asking for a deeper analysis of the problem or situation. Other case discussions may begin with small groups of four or five persons who read and discuss the case before they come to class. This is a way to prime the larger discussion group.

Teaching the Case

The first role of the teacher is to *probe* and thus clarify or even expand the contribution made by a participant. When someone makes a point in the discussion, the teachers may wish to focus on this insight and stay with the person as long as it seems helpful without being threatening. After a minute or so the discussion leader could then ask another student who has indicated that he or she wants to participate, "What do you think about that?" or "Do you agree with that statement?" This may also be useful when, in the course of the discussion, someone makes an exaggerated or misleading declaration. Rather than responding, the teacher may ask another student if he or she agrees. However, many case teachers have a working rule when teaching a case: on any issue there will always be a minority of at least *two*— the teacher and a person under attack. The instructor may need help at some point and the class is likely to be influenced by the previous teaching style. Style in case teaching clearly reveals the relationship between teacher and participants in the class.

Sometimes the teaching role will be that of a *referee*. As the discussion gets more lively, quite different opinions and even information may surface. A teacher may be tempted to avoid conflict or disagreement by looking for an easy or early consensus. We recommend not giving in to this temptation, since honest conflict is a great learning tool *if* the reasons for the difference of opinion are made clear. The instructor may even wish to heighten the conflict by saying, "John, that sounds just the opposite of what Kay was saying." "Fred you are frowning. Does that sound wrong to you?" However, the authors always try to stop conflict before it becomes warfare (a decision that comes with practice) by moving to the next issue.

The third job of the teacher is that of a *tour guide*. A tourist can muddle through the Acropolis on her own, but she will be more likely to appreciate the birthplace of Western culture if someone who has been there before guides her through. The best tour guides seem able to combine freedom with assistance. The class will be moving in its own way through the case, but they will need from time to time the services of a guide to make the visit richer. The teacher should help the class build on the suggestions of one another, sketch alternative solutions, and then compare them. As the learners under a good guide learn to trust and depend on one another, their learning will be multiplied and the benefit of the class increased.

Teaching Tools

Additional teaching tools which have been employed by other case teachers are listed here to suggest the variety of ways in which cases can be taught.

(1) ROLE PLAY. One method to draw participants into the case is to ask them temporarily to assume the roles of the persons in the case. The entire class might become a group of parents that Mary Johnson calls together to discuss the activities that went on in the parking lot and in the club party which Katie attended. A couple in the class might be asked to role play the discussion between Peter and Jane Murphy as they decide about their future, or between Sue Ann and a friend discussing abortion.

In each case, it appears best not to assign roles arbitrarily or ask for volunteers. Rather, many case teachers select persons they think would take the discussion seriously and make a contribution to the class. A teacher should ask if they would like to participate, but let them be free to say no. In a typical role play situation students come to the front of the class, sit across from each other, and then reconstruct what they think might have gone on in that discussion. After a couple of minutes, or as soon as the conversation becomes less than relevant, the teacher interrupts the conversation with a thank you or applause, and then asks the participants, "How did *you* feel about the conversation? Were you comfortable with what you said?" Only after they have shared, is the class asked what they learned from the role play or how they might have done it differently. A key to a good role play is to be always supportive of the participants who have risked themselves.

(2) VOTING. The dialogue may sometimes be focused or brought alive by the call for a vote on an issue that will be controversial. "How many think Sue Ann, given what you know now, should have the abortion?" "Who thinks Peter Murphy should reject the Peace Corps offer

and do what his father suggests?" The vote can be recorded after a show of hands. If persons are reluctant to take a position, they can be recorded as "undecided." A good teacher pushes people to decide and to defend their choice. Even a choice not to decide in a case like "The Dance of Life" has serious consequences for Sara, for no decision is a certain kind of choice. The best use of the vote is to probe for the reasons and assumptions that stand behind it. Sometimes, after a very good discussion, the authors take another vote to see if anyone has changed his or her mind. We ask why and can often note that the participants have really informed and persuaded one another.

(3) MONITORING. It almost always helps to keep track of the time devoted to the discussion of a particular question or to a role play. Warnings about time limits shared with the class, "Let us spend about five minutes on the issue . . . ," will allow a teacher to guide the progress of the case and to appropriately interrupt a learner who monopolizes the discussion. Learners will often develop their own skill at checking an over-talkative contributor or even encouraging a more reticent participant. A teacher might say, "Fred, you haven't had a chance to get in there yet. How do you feel about it?" Sensitive control is a way of demonstrating real care about the persons in the class.

(4) CHECKING DATA. One task of a good detective is to be accurate about the facts. The class should not speculate far beyond the data in the case or the class may get caught up in arguing about irrelevant issues. The role of the teacher is to remind the class to be responsible to the material in the case, even if their conclusions quite properly move out from the present position. The discussion leader may need to ask, "What evidence do you have that it might work?" A learner can then call on the case or personal experience to interpret his or her view. Other helpful techniques in case teaching are: eye contact with a participant (to encourage or alert him or her that the leader will be back, although it is not possible to call on her now) and body language (coming to stand beside a person to signal encouragement, or turning away to write on the board to signal "you have made your point"). This art of case-teaching style comes with practice and attention to checking data, and more important, checking the mood and interest level of the class.

(5) HONESTY. The integrity of the teacher is exposed in the case-study approach perhaps more than in other styles of teaching. Therefore it is important for a teacher to admit his or her own feelings about a situation in a case: "I am not clear about that issue myself." "I think it would be helpful to focus on Jane's relationship to Peter; she seems to be copping out." It is best not to role play an attitude or character unless this is first indicated to the class: "Let me be Mr. Murphy for a minute . . ." It may be necessary to gently rebuke a person who is purposely misleading the class or taking an outrageous position he or she doesn't really believe. Remember, when the teacher enters the discussion, his or her views are also subject to critique and rebuttal.

The discussion leader should not have any hesitation about saying, "I don't know the answer to that, let's work on it together." "I will do some digging before our next session, but there may not be a clear answer to that issue." An honest and open stance declares that one wants to share the responsibility for teaching and learning—that unusual but inevitable combination of a learcher.

Case Wrap-Up

At the conclusion of the discussion, the leader may wish to ask participants what they have learned from the case and from one another and then list these learnings. The teacher may also have important insights to add. If these are identified as personal concerns and not *the* solution, this may be an important contribution as well. A good leader avoids the temptation to try and trump the class with his or her insights. This tends to negate the learning process by diminishing the participants' accomplishments. Perhaps one could say, "This idea interests me and so I share it with you. Try it on and see if it fits the case. If not, discard it."

Satisfaction in the case-study approach comes if it meets the goals of both teacher and learner. The authors believe the case method contributes to *wisdom* as learners integrate and relate the content or theory of the reading to their practice or experience in daily life. It fosters *maturity* as participants learn to be responsible for their own decisions and to understand the reasons and consequences of a decision they choose to defend. Finally, the process may *build skills* in analysis of a situation, in creative exploration of alternatives, and in the ability to articulate and reflect upon one's own and others' values.

In conclusion, the authors acknowledge our debt to our colleagues, the Staff and Fellows of the Case-Study Institute, who in creative ways have struggled since 1971 to employ and adapt the classic case-study method of institutions like Harvard Business School and Harvard Law School to the teaching of theology. The class procedure and practical aids cited above have been "class-tested" by these colleagues and are recommended to you through their experience and critique. Special thanks go to Ann D. Meyers and Louis Weeks for their previous writing and sharing on the teaching of cases upon which we have so freely drawn.

May your skill and sensitivity as case teacher, learner, and co-learcher increase with practice.

RESOURCE GUIDE TO INTRODUCTION

A. Study Questions

1. As you begin the study of Christianity, can you think of ways the Christian tradition has affected the American culture in terms of ethics, music, or art? Consider Negro spirituals ("Swing Low, Sweet Chariot," "Jacob's Ladder"), contemporary songs ("Morning Has Broken"), or the phrase on our coins, "In God We Trust." Also refer to Frances Harmon's *Religious Freedom in America* (see bibliography) for this question. Look through any book on the history of art; try to evaluate the influence of Christianity on the development of art.

2. What are some of the Christian values? Where do you think they came from? Has the value system of the Christian religion had any effect on modern politics or on public reaction to government policies? What kind of effects do you see?

3. From your study of world history, have you seen ways in which the Christian church has modified specific historical and political events? (Consider the Crusades, Renaissance, concept of "Manifest Destiny," etc.) Can you think of historical or contemporary figures who were willing to make great sacrifices or even to die for their beliefs and values? (Consider Joan of Arc, Sir Thomas More, Dietrich Bonhoeffer, Albert Schweitzer, Martin Luther King.)

4. How do you define the word "religion"? Who do you think of as a "religious person"? Do you think of yourself as religious? Why?

5. What person, thing, or idea are you committed to? What is meant by "ultimate concern"? What is your own ultimate concern? How do you show this in your actions, thoughts, and beliefs? Can you say what your best friend's ultimate concern is? What would he or she say was your ultimate concern?

6. Do you consider yourself Christian or know those who consider

themselves Christian? How can you tell if a person is a Christian? What do you understand to be signs or criteria for being Christian?

7. What does it mean to be part of a "community"? To what kind of communities do you belong? How would you explain the concept of Christian community? From the Christian perspective, why is it not possible to become "fully human" alone?

B. Suggested Activities

1. Consider using some of the rank order exercises in Sidney Simon's *Values Clarification*, p. 58 (see Bibliography). The Bible suggests the basic Christian values are faith, hope, and love. In light of the rank order exercise, think about your own personal choices. What values influence the choices you make? Where did these values come from? How many of these values could be characterized as Christian values?

2. In reference to study question #3, a small group might reflect on or research the activities of Daniel and Phillip Berrigan, and consider how these men illustrate the concept of ultimate concern and a "lived faith." Another group could report on some of the traditional elements in the beliefs of "conscientious objectors."

3. In reference to study question #6, make a list of the ten persons, things, or ideas that are the most important to you now. Then rank these items in order of importance in helping you make decisions. Discuss how this exercise might indicate the relative importance of personal values for decision-making.

4. Lyman Coleman (see Bibliography) suggests an exercise entitled "In the Event of Fire" in which participants list the first ten things they would grab if their house caught on fire and they had only three minutes to get out before everything burned (e.g., guitar, bankbook, scrapbook). Then number these items in order of importance. Finally, select only five items and jot down why these are important (e.g., economic value, spiritual, senti-

mental). Discuss these choices in light of what they reveal about values.

C. Audio-Visual Materials*

Filmstrip: "The Great Mystique Shatterer" made by Franciscan Communication Center, 1229 Santee St., Los Angeles, CA 90015. Rental: $15.00. Fifty strip filmstrip presents different representations of Jesus from great art works of many cultures. This is an excellent film for use with or without soundtrack.

Film: "Moment to Act" 16mm film, 29 minutes, black and white, guide, 1962, National Council of Churches. Available from denominational and public libraries. Rental: $8.00. A young woman, home from a mental institution, explores the lack of understanding in those around her and the breach between their statements of belief and the "living out" of these ideals. The film is excellent for discussion.

D. Bibliography

Lyman Coleman, *Discovery, A Mini Course in Christian Community* (Waco, Texas: Word, 1972) "In Event of Fire," pp. 14, 27–28. Suggests many other creative exercises which help the participants evaluate their priorities and values. Text is specifically Christian oriented.

Francis S. Harmon, *Religious Freedom in America* (New York: Friendship Press, 1973). This pamphlet can be ordered from Interchurch Center, 475 Riverside Dr., New York, NY 10027. Excellent resource booklet and study guide on the effect and importance of religious traditions in the United States.

Richard Niebuhr, *Christ and Culture* (New York: Harper & Row Torchbook, 1951). Classic analysis of Christianity in dialogue with culture and their effect on one another.

Sidney Simon, L. Howe, H. Kirschenbaum, *Values Clarification, A*

---

*In locating any of the films recommended in this guide, before writing to the distributor, first contact religious film libraries, public libraries, and denominational church libraries in your area. Rental fees vary.

Handbook of Practical Strategies for Teachers and Students (New York: Hart, 1972). Exercises for value clarification.

John B. Noss, *Man's Religions* (New York: Macmillan, 1974). See General Bibliography. A good section on primitive and traditional religions. Section One, pp. 2–77.

Ninian Smart, *The Religious Experience of Mankind* (New York: Scribner, 1968). See General Bibliography. An excellent introduction on the meaning of religion. Chapter I, pp. 3–23.

Paul Tillich, *Dynamics of Faith* (New York: Harper & Row, 1957). Defines and develops the classic understanding of religion as ultimate concern, the meaning of faith, and the importance of Christian symbols.

James K. Uphoff, "Religion in our Culture and Curriculum." Write to PERSC, Wright State University, Dayton, OH 45431. A very interesting, brief monograph containing cartoons and news articles which can provide a good basis for discussion of the frequent reference to religion in mass media.

RESOURCE GUIDE TO CASE STUDY A:
"A MATTER OF LIFE AND DEATH"

A. Suggestions for Teaching the Case

1. Begin your discussion of the case where the story ends. A decision is demanded. What will Sue Ann do? What should she do? If you were a friend of Sue Ann's like Sharon, or a friend of Danny's, what would you advise them to do and why?

2. Discuss each of the persons involved in the case, (Danny, parents, Dr. Engles). What is their relationship to Sue Ann? Are any of the people involved *responsible* for anyone else in the case? Why or why not? Consider role playing a scene between Sue Ann and Danny, Sharon, or Connie Davies. Two persons in the class might take the parts of these characters and share in a conversation for three or four minutes. How much do you know about each of these people? What are you assuming about them? Does this help to give you further insights into the problem facing Sue Ann? Are there factors in this situation, like pressure from the culture or degree of maturity, that you have overlooked?

3. Consider the implications of both decisions (to abort or to have the baby) for Sue Ann. The participants might vote on which decision Sue Ann should make (knowing only what we know from the case). The teacher could record the vote and then ask each person to support his or her choice. What are the important values in making any of these decisions? List the reasons for and against each decision.

4. "I came that you might have life and have it abundantly." "Love your neighbor as yourself." How could these biblical quotations from the "Introduction" speak to Sue Ann's decision? How can Christianity affect how one feels about the worth and quality of life? What do you think is the basis of the official Ro-

man Catholic position on abortion? (Consider the statement, "Man has no right to extinguish the potential life of the fetus which is a gift of God the Creator.") What would be the religious basis on which a Christian could responsibly decide to have an abortion? (Consider the statement, "In a conflict over the quality and fullness of life for the baby or the parents, God gives us the right and responsibility to make a wise decision that contributes to the quality of all human life.")

5. Why is Sue Ann reluctant to share her problem? Could other persons (friends, school counselors) or a community support her and Danny in making a decision they can both live with? Are there any other options besides keeping the baby?

6. How do recent Supreme Court decisions, which allow abortion under certain conditions, affect this case now that it is legal to have an abortion during the first months of pregnancy? Do the civil laws affect the moral questions involved? Why or why not?

B. Suggested Activities

1. Secure the statements of several church positions from the "Right to Life" Organization, 2201 Paul Spring Parkway, Alexandria, VA 22308, and from the Religious Coalition for Abortion Rights, 100 Maryland Avenue, N.E., Washington, DC 20002.

2. Form several discussion groups and assign a major position to each group, xeroxing a copy only of the position they are to defend. Hold a debate with each group, setting three minutes to defend their view and one minute rebuttal. Afterwards, each group could cite strengths and weaknesses of the position they defended.

3. Do some research on the current legal standing for "abortion on demand" in your own state. What is the current U.S. Supreme Court ruling? What are the counseling services for abortion in your town or community?

C. Audio-Visual Suggestions

1. "The Bird," 16mm film, 3 minutes, color, Fred Wolf. Available from Contemporary Films, 838 Custer Avenue, Evanston IL 60202. Rental: $10.00. A bird brings a man and a woman together. When the man is finished with the woman, he finishes off the bird too. Good cartoon satire on the sexual mores of our modern society. Open-ended, it allows much room for discussion on the quality of relationships.

2. "Sex: A Moral Dilemma for Teenagers," two sound filmstrips, 16mm, Part 1—16 minutes, Part 2—15 minutes, color, 1966. Guidance Associates, 23 Washington Ave., Pleasantville, NY 10570. Sale: $35.00 with records, $39.00 with cassettes. Teens speak for themselves. This film is good for information as well as a catalyst for discussing pregnancy outside of marriage and communication barriers between parent and child.

3. "Sex Is a Beautiful Thing," 16mm film, 28 minutes, color, 1970, Family Films 5823 Santa Monica Blvd., Hollywood, CA 90038. Rental: $20.00. Two college age couples consider premarital sex within a Christian context. We recommend this film for "trying on the Christian glasses," and find the dialogue stimulating for further discussion.

NOTE: If you are seeking a balanced portrayal of the abortion issue which understands both sides, we would suggest you avoid the use of highly polemical films only, such as those supplied by "Right to Life" or "Abortion on Demand" groups.

RESOURCE GUIDE TO CHAPTER 1

A. Study Questions

1. Is the Bible merely history? What else is it?

2. Have you known or do you know anyone who has had their attitudes shaped or changed by the Bible? Why do you think the Bible is so often quoted by people? Do they use it correctly? How would you know?

3. Compare the two Genesis accounts of Creation (Genesis 1 and 2 and 3). There is a seeming paradox. Humanity is good. Why? Humanity is basically evil. Why? Based on your own interpretation of the creation stories, how could you reconcile these differences?

4. In reading the "second" creation story (Genesis 2:4b–3:24) how does the account of the serpent illustrate "the problem of human existence?" How does a person's disobedience "separate" him or her from God? How can you become "separated from" another person by breaking a promise? How do you "restore" that relationship? Could Sue Ann's choice for *or* against the abortion "separate" her from God or another person?

5. In what ways can freedom of choice increase one's level of responsibility? How does this apply to Sue Ann? Would this also apply to Dr. Engles? Are you really free to make major decisions about how you live your life, or is that only an illusion? What restraints or boundaries do you have through parents, friends, or demands of culture? What is the basis of being "really free"? Give an example. Can you be free and responsible at the same time?

6. What is meant by a covenant? How is a covenant "broken" and then "renewed"? How do Christians understand Christ as the "New Covenant"? (See Hebrews 8:6–13) Did Sue Ann and Danny have a covenant? Did they have one with their parents?

Will their decision affect their relationship to each other and to their parents?

7. Read a copy of the traditional Christian marriage vows. In what ways can these be understood as a covenant? What kind of promises are important to you? Do other people trust you to keep your promises? How does this shape your relationship to other people? For what reasons do you keep promises or break them? Give an illustration.

8. What does the word "prophet" mean? How would you apply the criticisms of the ancient Old Testament prophets like Amos (Amos 5:11–15) and Jeremiah (Jeremiah 25:1–7) to the present world situation? What were they trying to tell the people? What was their primary goal? How does our society treat the poor and oppressed? Name a modern prophet. How do you respond to her or him? (See activity #4.)

9. For an interesting summary of the Christian understanding of the Old Testament, read Acts: 7:1–53, in which Stephen addresses the Jewish elders. Who is the Righteous One? How would you compare the Exodus with the coming of the Messiah? What was the purpose of the Old and the New Covenants? How did the people respond? How does the New Covenant relate to Sue Ann and Danny?

B. Suggested Activities and Projects

1. Research some of the Old Testament Convants between God and
   a) Noah (Genesis 6–9)
   b) Abraham (Genesis 17)
   c) Jacob (Genesis 35)
   d) the Israelite Nation (Exodus 24)
   For this study consider using a translation such as the New English Bible which many persons find easier to read than the King James or the Revised Standard Versions.

2. Should you decide not to utilize any of the suggested films on the development of the Bible, research and report on a) the canoni-

zation of the current books, b) the use of the Bible in the Middle Ages, c) the spread and historical influence of the translation of the Bible into the vernacular and, d) the more modern translations of the Bible.

3. Have different groups read and report on specific stories in the Bible; e.g., Genesis 22:1–8; 2 Samuel 11–12; John 8:1–11; John 11:1–53. What do these stories say about the relationship between humankind and God?

4. Use the Periodicals Index to research current articles listed under "prophet," keeping in mind the distinction between a fortune teller and a religious prophet.

5. Write a general outline of the early history of the Jews. Discuss the ways in which Christianity is linked to Judaism.

6. Some Christians understand the Bible as literal, others view it as symbolic or a combination of the two. Have individuals or groups prepare a report on this issue based on interviews with Christians supporting different positions.

C. Audio-Visual Suggestions

1. "The Antkeeper," 16mm film, 30 minutes, color, 1967, Lutheran Church in America. Available from LCA Board of Publication Films Dept., 2900 Queen Lane, Philadelphia, PA 19129. Rental: $25.00. Also available in many denominational libraries. Rental varies. An allegorical account of God's relationship to humanity through Christ, this is a provocative and controversial film.

2. "Creation," sound filmstrip, 7 minutes, color, 1970, Broadman Films. Available from (Southern) Baptist Bookstores, or 127 Ninth Ave. N., Nashville, TN 37203. Sale: $7.50. Has beautiful photography. This is a good film to introduce a discussion of the relationship between God, humankind, and the creation covenant.

3. "The Search for Black Identity: Martin Luther King," set of two sound filmstrips, 15 minutes each, color, with records. Available from Guidance Associates, 23 Washington Ave., Pleasantville, NY 10570. Sale: records, $35.00; cassette, $39.00.

This film is good for a discussion of the Christian basis for the non-violent civil rights movement as well as a consideration of King as modern day prophet. This film could also be well utilized with Chapter 1 to consider a "lived faith."

4. "Our Bible: How It Came to Us," 3 filmstrips, black and white, guide. Order from American Bible Society, 1865 Broadway, New York, NY 10023. Rental: $8.00 each or $22.50 for all three: (1) The Formation of the Bible, (2) The Bible Spreads Across Europe, (3) The Making of the English Bible. These can be ordered separately. A related series of four shorter filmstrips entitled "How Our Bible Came to Us" (also American Bible Society) costs $15.00 to purchase the sound filmstrip; this set contains an excellent guide.

D. Bibliography

Books

Yohanan Aharoni and Michael Avi-Yonah, *The Macmillan Bible Atlas* (New York: Macmillan, 1968). A thorough atlas for use in both Old and New Testament references. Good supplemental text.

John Bright, *A History of Israel* (Philadelphia: Westminster, 1959). Excellent work which traces in detail the historical development of the Israelite nation.

Robert McAfee Brown, *The Bible Speaks to You* (Philadelphia: Westminster, 1955). A readable little book based on the theme of the relevance of the Bible for today. Clearly and simply explains Christian concepts.

Martin Buber, *The Prophetic Faith* (New York: Harper & Row Torchbook, 1973). Displays insight into the central events and forces of Israel's religion by one of the foremost Jewish interpreters of scripture.

Reginald Fuller and G. Ernest Wright, *Book of the Acts of God* (New York: Doubleday, 1957). Widely read introduction to the Bible.

B. Davie Napier, *From Faith to Faith* (New York: Harper & Brothers, 1955). Considers the basic, underlying themes of the Old Testament as a means of understanding the New Testament.

Though now out of print, this is a text found in most religious libraries.

R. B. Scott, *The Relevance of the Prophets* (New York: Macmillan, 1969). A good treatment of the leading forces and themes in prophecy and of their importance for our generation.

RESOURCE GUIDE TO CHAPTER 2

A. Study Questions

1. Why is the New Testament particularly important to Christians?

2. The Gospel writers were selective in what they wrote about Jesus (refer to John 20:30–31 and John 21:25). What was their purpose in writing? Would you want to know anything about Jesus that the Gospel writers did not include? Why?

3. This chapter contains many references to Jesus. From the separate stories listed, what do you "know" about this man? How would you describe him to someone else? Give specific examples of his actions and words to support your description.

4. Discuss how a Christian might answer the following two questions: (1) What do the actions and teachings of Jesus say about the kind of relationship you should have with other persons? (2) What does your relationship to other people say about your relation to God? Can you turn that question around? What is the *quality* of the relationship between Sue Ann and Danny?

5. Discuss the statement, "Jesus is the one person who is 'fully human.'" What makes him unique?

6. Discuss the meaning of the kingdom of God. Is this a political kingdom? What are some of the guidelines for this kingdom? Refer to the Sermon on the Mount, Matthew 5. Has this kingdom come yet?

7. What does the "incarnation" mean? [Note: the word is from the Latin *incarnari,* to be made flesh.] Why is this important to Christians?

8. Many Christians understand Christ's death as God's gift and sacrifice for humanity. How would you interpret his death? What were some religious and political factors which led to Jesus' crucifixion?

9. Throughout this chapter, when events in the life of Christ are

mentioned, the authors have used the past tense (e.g. Jesus was born; he spoke; he acted). However, many other statements about Jesus use the present tense (e.g., "to know who Jesus *is*"). Why do Christians speak of Jesus in the present tense? What does this reveal about their understanding of God's relationship to humanity? (Refer to Hebrews 7:22–29)

10. Why is the resurrection crucial to the Christian understanding of the New Covenant? (Refer to Paul in 1 Corinthians 15:12–28)

11. It has been said that to believe that Jesus is the divine Son of God depends on personal experience and not on reason. Discuss why you would support or deny this statement.

B. Suggested Activities and Projects

1. The miracles of Jesus are understood by some Christians as symbolic and by others as actual fact. With the use of a synoptic (comparative) Gospel account compare the different Gospel versions of several miracles. Consider the purpose of the different authors in telling these stories.

2. Do miracles, in the biblical sense, happen today, or were they pre-scientific? Interview a Christian science healer to report on this particular Christian concept of healing. Research what many Christians mean by "faith healing."

3. Conduct further research on the political and religious background during the time of Christ. How might this have influenced Jesus' crucifixion? (One biblical reference would be John 11:45–52.) How did Jesus antagonize both the religious and political leaders in his day? References for this project are cited in the bibliography.

C. Suggested Additional Case Study

How do Christians follow the example of Christ's life in situations never addressed in the Bible? As a way to discuss this question, consider using the case study, "Westport Grass," in which a church youth leader is called into a family crisis related to drugs. "Westport Grass" also raises the issue of a Christian's responsibility to individuals as well as to the society. The case and a study guide can be found in Louis and Carolyn Weeks and Robert and Alice Evans, *Casebook for Christian Living* (Atlanta: John Knox, 1977), pp. 94–99, or the case alone can be ordered directly from the Intercollegiate Case Clearing House, Soldier's Field, Boston, MA 02163.

D. Audio-Visual Suggestions

Films

1. "The Guide," 16mm, 30 minutes, color, 1964. Cathedral Films, 2921 W. Alameda Ave., Box 1608, Burbank, CA 91505. Rental: $16.00. A contemporary presentation of Christ's life with modern photography of Palestine, this film is excellent for discussion of the relevance of Christ's teachings for today's living.
2. "Parable," 16mm film, 22 minutes, color, 1964. Council of Churches of N.Y.C. Available from Council of Churches, Suite 456, 475 Riverside Drive, New York, NY 10027. Rental: $35.00. This is a thought-provoking film of the Christ portrayed as a clown affecting changes in the lives of those around him. It was very well received in field testing.
3. "Right Here, Right Now," 16mm film, 15 minutes, color, 1970. St. Francis Productions. Available from TeleKETICS, 1229 S. Santee St., Los Angeles, CA 90015. Rental: $14.00; super 8mm, rental: $12.00. This story of a janitor who affects other people through his love is good for discussion of the concept of Christ's "presence."
4. "Son of Man" (The Last Days of Jesus Christ), David Potter, 16mm film, 96 minutes (2 reels), black and white, BBC-TV. Available through numerous film libraries. This challenging film, which has received international critical acclaim and strong reviews by high school students and teachers, is accompanied by a good set of study questions.

Records

1. "Jesus Christ Superstar," Decca Records, 1970. The album includes a script. This contemporary interpretation of Christ's life

and death is good for discussion of the roles of Judas and Pilate, and of Christ's understanding of his own mission.

2. "Rich Man and Lazarus," 33 1/3 rpm record, or tape cassette, Koinonia Records. Sale: $3.98 record, $4.50 cassette. This is an exciting contemporary retelling of three of Jesus' parables.

E. Bibliography

Roland H. Bainton, *Christendom,* Vol. I (New York: Harper Torchbook, 1966). Contains a clear account of the historical and political background for Christianity. Chapters I and II.

John Bright, *The Kingdom of God* (Nashville: Abingdon, 1953). Explores the biblical concept of the kingdom of God and its meaning for the church.

Günther Bornkamm, *Jesus of Nazareth* (New York: Harper & Row, 1961). One of the most readable of the treatments of the life of Jesus which is well-grounded in scholarship. Solid but not exciting.

Frederick Buechner, *Wishful Thinking: A Theological A B C* (New York: Harper & Row, 1973). A very readable little book with a contemporary exposition of many Christian concepts.

Reginald Fuller, *Interpreting the Miracles* (Philadelphia: Westminster, 1963). Careful analysis of the miracles from a well known biblical scholar.

Joachim Jeremias, *The Parables of Jesus* (New York: Scribner, Lyceum Ed., 1971). One of the best modern treatments of the parables by a noted German New Testament scholar.

Robert M. Montgomery and William R. Stegner, *Two-Source Theory and the Synoptic Gospels* (Nashville: Abingdon, 1970). Part of the Auxiliary Studies in the Bible Series by Abingdon Press. A work book with experiences to show how the Gospels were formed.

Harold H. Rowley, ed. *New Atlas of the Bible* (Garden City: Doubleday & Co, 1969). Clearly written pictorial account of the historical situation during the time of Jesus.

Burton Throckmorton, ed. *Gospel Parallels* (New York: Nelson, 1957). A standard synopsis of the first three Gospels.

Copies of the New Testament would be helpful for further study in

Chapters 2 and 3. If you do not have a set of classroom Bibles, paperback copies of the New Testament *(Good News for Modern Man)* can be acquired for 36¢ each from the American Bible Society, 1865 Broadway, New York, NY 10023. The order number is 02810.

RESOURCE GUIDE TO CASE STUDY B: "SERVICE OR SACRIFICE"

A. Suggestions for Teaching the Case

1. First try to clarify the basic issues involved in this case. A possible way to do this is for one participant to imagine that he is Peter Murphy trying to explain the decision to his cousin Ed, a junior in high school. How would he tell this to Ed? What reasons would he give for either decision? Also consider how Peter might tell the same thing to his parish pastor.

2. In previous chapters the notion of "responsibility" has been mentioned. What do you think this word means? Where does Peter's responsibility lie? Why might he feel responsible for anyone other than himself? What influence do you think the Christian faith has on Peter?

3. When Jane asserts, "We are mature enough to make up our own minds," how do you think she feels? Now that she is married, does she have further responsibility to or for her parents? Do you think she is being responsible to Peter? Why or why not? Is there any way in which she could be more helpful to Peter, or has she helped as much as she can?

4. From what you have learned about him in this case, how would you describe Mr. Murphy? Why do you think he wants Peter to reconsider his initial decision to enter the Peace Corps? How would Peter be better prepared to serve others if he waits until later to join the Peace Corps?

5. Discuss what it means to be "*in* but not *of* the world." How would Peter Murphy's decision relate to this concept? Is Peter faithful or just foolish? Are there any alternative decisions for Peter besides the immediate answer? Why or why not? What does the title of this case mean to you?

6. What do you think Peter means when he tells Jane that this decision could determine the rest of their lives? Whichever deci-

sion Peter makes, what are the *implications* of that decision? What are some of the underlying values behind each decision? What would you advise him to tell the Peace Corps and his father?

7. Do you know anyone who seems totally dedicated to one endeavor (e.g., sports, work, or grades)? Are you committed to any causes?

8. Do you presently have beliefs for which you would be willing to give two years of your life? Is the price too high?

B. Suggested Activities

1. Sometimes commitments mean sacrifice. An excellent exercise to work on this concept is in Gerri Curwin's *Search for Values*, (Dayton: Pflaum/Standard, 1972) entitled, "The Jailer," p. 75. Fill out this sheet and discuss your answers. This exercise could be a good introduction to the case study on "Service or Sacrifice."

2. Write to the Peace Corps or Vista (812 Connecticut Avenue, Washington DC 20525) or use their toll free phone number for available information on the Peace Corps and Vista (Volunteers in Service to America). Discuss why these government programs may or may not fit into the Christian concept of "service." In what ways do they involve "sacrifice" for the participants?

C. Audio-Visual Suggestions

1. "Now What?" 16mm film, 12 minutes, color, 1970, Board of College Education and Church Vocations of the Lutheran Church in America. Available from Contemporary/McGraw Hill Films, 828 Custer Ave., Evanston, IL 60202. Rental: $17.00. This film can lead to good discussion of issues of materialism and lifestyle.

2. "That's Me," 16mm film, 15 minutes, black and white, Walker Stewart. Mass Media Ministries, 2116 N. Charles St., Baltimore, MD 21218, and local libraries. Rental: $15.00. Alan Arkin portrays a high school dropout in a provocative discussion

with a social worker. It is good for further discussion of contemporary values and personal identity.

RESOURCE GUIDE TO CHAPTER 3

A. Study Questions

1. Pentecost is a day of celebration in many Christian churches. What happened in the early church at the first Pentecost? (See Acts 2.) Why was this so important?

2. What do Christians mean when they refer to the Holy Spirit?

3. Reread the conversion experience of Paul and the events which followed (Acts 9:1–31). Why was Saul persecuting the Christians? How do you explain the reaction of the Christians to Paul's change? Why were the Jewish leaders so angry with Paul? What would your response be to someone who suddenly changed the direction of his or her lifestyle?

4. Have you read or heard of modern conversions? How do people explain the change which comes over them? In many parts of North America there has been a revival of interest in the meaning of the presence of the Holy Spirit. Do you see any parallels between elements of the contemporary "Jesus Revolution" and the witness of the early church in the New Testament? (See Project #1.)

5. What do you understand to be the "mission" of the church? What is the biblical basis for your interpretation? (See Luke 4:18–19, Matt. 28:19–20.) Why do you think Christians accept this mission? What is Peter Murphy's interpretation of this mission? How is his decision to enter or not to enter the Peace Corps at this time influenced by his understanding of the mission or vision of the church?

6. How do Christians explain why persons fail in this mission? Some Christians suggest reasons such as: because of God's gift of freedom; because they are not allowing themselves to be led by the Holy Spirit; or because they are unwilling or unable to respond to what they think God requires of them. How do you respond to these answers?

7. Discuss the statement, "In the early church being a Christian made it imperative that one also be a member of the Christian

community." Discuss why some Christians would affirm this. Do you agree with these reasons for having a church community: (1) mutual support and strength; (2) learning about Jesus; (3) fulfilling the goals of service to others; (4) sharing with others to enable self-evaluation and change?

8. How do the symbols of the vine and the body of Christ symbolize the community of believers?

9. "I become what I truly am only in relation to another person." How could the decision before Peter and Jane be related to this statement? What is their "community of support"? How does Peter see his life in relationship to other persons? How would either decision he might make relate to this idea?

10. Discuss the ways in which Christianity is very different from Judaism.

11. In contrast to the strict Jewish law, the theology of Paul stresses the freedom which Christ promises:

   Christ set us free, to be free men. . . . When you seek to be justified by way of law, . . .you have fallen out of the domain of God's grace. For to us, our hope of attaining that righteousness which we eagerly await is the work of the Spirit through faith. Galatians 5:1–5 NEB

   What do you think Paul means by saying "Christ set us free"? Free from what?

12. Many American Negro spirituals such as "Go Down Moses" and "Swing Low, Sweet Chariot" contain eloquent statements of faith and also subtle implications that the concept of "freedom" promised by Christ has very practical implications. Study the words of these songs: do you think they have a double meaning?

B. Suggested Activities and Projects

1. Does the Holy Spirit speak to Christians today in the same dramatic ways as in the early church? There are many testimonials by Pentecostals, "Jesus Freaks," and members of the charismatic movement which affirm the dramatic effects of the Holy Spirit on people's lives today. The bibliography suggests a number of

books for reports on this phenomenon. Consult the *Periodicals Index* for recent articles.

2. Research some of the basic symbols of the Christian church (e.g., cross, dove, fish, flame, keys, lamb, or the grapes and wheat). Investigate the history of each symbol and try to analyze which aspects of the Christian faith each symbol conveys.

3. In the medieval period when the vast majority of people could not read, the Christian message was conveyed by pictures and later through stained glass. Visit churches or a cathedral in your community with notable stained glass windows and study the symbols. Discuss why these symbols might or might not be important today. A good resource for this study would be Ireland's *Textile Art in the Church*. See bibliography.

C. Audio-Visual Materials

1. "Bewilderblissed," 16mm film, 13 minutes, color, guide, 1970, Lutheran Church in America from LCA Board of Publications. Rental: $10.00. Focusing initially on the Tower of Babel event, the film deals in an exciting and appealing way with the concept of the Holy Spirit joining Christians in a common mission.

2. "Between the Dark and the Daylight," 16mm film, 28 minutes, color, 1969, Church World Service, 475 Riverside Drive, New York, NY 10027. Available from denominational film libraries. Also available from Augsburg Films, 426 S. Fifth Street, Minneapolis, MN 55415. Rental: approx. $8.00. This exciting and informative film contrasts the "darkness" of much of the world in need and the "daylight" of the world of plenty. It can be used to stimulate conversation about how and why individuals serve in impoverished areas.

3. "Charismatic Renewal," 16mm film, 15 minutes, TeleKET-ICS. Available from Franciscan Communications Center, 1229 South Santee Street, Los Angeles, CA 90015. Rental: $15.00. This is a documentary on Catholic Pentecostalism.

4. "It's About This Carpenter," 16mm film, 14 minutes, black and white, 1964. Available from New York University Film Library, 26 Washington Place, New York, NY 10003. Rental: $10.00.

This symbolic portrayal of humanity's relation to Christ and the church is based on a New York carpenter delivering a cross to a church.

5. "Parable," (see reference in Chapter 2 Resource Guide). This film can be quite effective for a study of contemporary use of symbolism.

6. "Yaane," 16mm film, 20 minutes, color, 1972, available from Lay Mission-Helpers Association, 1531 West Ninth Street, Los Angeles, CA 90015. Rental: free. In seeing this beautifully photographed and fascinating view of African village life and the modern mission of the Christian church, viewers should be aware that this is a recruitment film for mission workers. It is a provocative film for discussion of stewardship of life and the motivating factors which lead some Christians into foreign mission service. Request the free brochure for helpful background comments on the title, places, and persons in the film.

D. Bibliography

Rudolf Bultmann, *Theology of the New Testament,* 2 volumes (New York: Scribner, 1970). Difficult reading, but a modern classic, especially good on the treatment of Paul's theology.

Adolf Deissmann, *Paul* (New York: Harper Torchbook, 1957). Written with the fascination of a travel book. Presents Paul as a vital person.

C. H. Dodd, *The Meaning of Paul for Today* (Cleveland, Ohio: Collins-World Publications, 1978). Instructive interpretation of Paul's life and thought, with good scholarly foundation.

R. Enroth, E. Erickson, C. Peters, *Jesus People: Old Time Religion in the Age of Aquarius* (Grand Rapids: Eerdmans, 1972). One of the more comprehensive and objective studies of the Jesus movement.

Michael Harper, *A New Way of Living* (Plainfield, N. J.: Logos International, 1973). Tells the story of the Church of the Redeemer in Houston, Texas, which was radically changed by the Holy Spirit. Provides insight into the charismatic movement.

Marion P. Ireland, *Textile Art in the Church* (Nashville: Abingdon,

1971). A fine discussion of Christian symbols and artwork from the early church to modern times. See especially pp. 85–106. Beautiful photographs.

John L. Sherrill, *They Speak with Other Tongues* (New York: Pyramid, 1967). Popular basic book on the charismatic movement.

J. Weiss, *The History of Primitive Christianity*, 2 vols. (New York: Harper & Row Torchbook). Careful and scholarly work on history of the apostolic age.

RESOURCE GUIDE TO CHAPTER 4

A. Study Questions

1. Try and develop a general overview of this chapter. Use the subtitles as a guide.

2. Discuss the ways in which an understanding of the Bible has influenced the development of the church. In your discussion you might consider: (1) Jesus' Great Commission (Matthew 28:18–20); (2) the impact that the concept of "Christ as Lord" has had on the political persecutions of the church, plus its influence on Augustine and Aquinas; (3) establishment of the Pope as Peter's successor (Matthew 16:18); (4) influence on the Reformation (Romans 1:17 and Ephesians 2:8–10); (5) influence on the concept of church unity (John 17:20–23).

3. How would you describe the life of the early Christians in Rome (first and second century)? What were the political and religious reasons for their persecution? Do you see any parallels between the early persecution of the Christians and that of the Jews in Nazi Germany? Are there countries today where Christians must meet secretly? (A suggested research topic.) What would Christians do to share and serve if the practice of Christianity were outlawed in the U.S.?

4. Discuss what many of the Crusaders might have understood as the "Lordship of Christ." How does this relate to the fears of the Jewish and Roman leaders responsible for the death of the "King of the Jews?" What did Jesus mean when he said, "My kingdom is not of this world?" (Read John 18:36.)

5. What are some of the major religious issues which have divided Christians during the historical development of Christianity? In your discussion consider the elements which caused the split in the Eastern Orthodox and Roman Catholic Church and the basic issues of the Reformation.

6. What do you see as themes running through the history of the church?

7. In what ways can the history of the church be a resource for the contemporary church? Can we learn anything from the tragedies

of the historical church, such as the Crusades? Does the history of the church provide a standard for how Christians should act today? Would the demand to "love your enemies" be a good guide to success and happiness?

8. Paul was quoted as saying, "There are many parts, yet one body." (1 Corinthians 12:20 RSV) How can this be used as an argument for the many denominational divisions within the church, if the church is understood as the "body of Christ"? Do you think the teachings of Jesus support this kind of division?

9. Discuss what it means to be "*in* but not *of* the world," a guideline for Christians for many centuries (one of many general references: John 17:13–19). How would Peter Murphy's decision relate to this concept?

B. Suggested Projects and Activities

As this chapter of necessity only briefly touches on several significant religious persons and events, it can provide an excellent opportunity for individual research projects and reports.

1. Investigate life in the catacombs of Rome and the secret symbols that Christians designed (e.g., the fish). There are also a number of recent magazine articles on the topic of modern day persecutions of Christians in Uganda and Korea. Consult the Periodicals Index.

2. Heresies: (a) Research some of the more prominent heresies of the early church: the Gnostics, Marcionites, Arians. How did the Apostles' or Nicene creeds counter these positions? Why did the church see these heresies as dangerous? (b) Research the modern heresy trial of Bishop Pike. What was his position and why did some members in the Episcopal Church declare his position heretical?

3. The architecture of the medieval cathedral is a remarkable achievement. Research the significance of the shape of the sanctuary, the placement of the altar and pulpit, and the use of statues. Why are there so many pictures in the early churches? Compare this to the architecture of a modern Protestant and a modern Roman Catholic Church. What do the differences tell you about how

the church speaks to different generations? What characteristics remained the same? Why?

4. Research both the political and religious forces behind the Protestant Reformation movement in Germany. Why did this movement spread so fast in Western Europe?

5. Investigate how men like Henry VIII of England, John Calvin of Geneva, and John Knox of Scotland affected both the religious and political directions of their time? In what ways is their influence felt today? Research the influence John Calvin's form of church and city government had on the basic elements of American governmental structure.

6. Other topics for reports could be the monastic movement, the Inquisition, the political power of the popes in the Middle Ages, Martin Luther, the World Council of Churches, or the current trend toward church unity in Canada and the U.S.

7. Research the famous Scopes Trial in Tennessee. How does Darwin's work challenge scriptural interpretations? There are cities and counties in the U.S. today where Darwin's work is banned. What are the religious reasons for this? Why do some Christians reject Darwin's thesis? How do other Christians defend his thesis on religious grounds.

C. Audio-Visual Suggestions

1. "Icons," 16mm film, 14 minutes, color. Available from the International Film Bureau, 332 S. Michigan Ave., Chicago, IL. 60604. Rental: $15.00. Containing examples of fifteenth to nineteenth century religious paintings of the Eastern Christian Church, this film traces the development of icons both as an art form and as a reflection of historical change.

2. "Martin Luther," sound filmstrip, 73 frames, black and white, script, guide, 1955. Concordia Films, 3558 S. Jefferson Ave., St. Louis, MO 63118. Also available from denominational film libraries. Sale: $10.00 with record. Taken from the feature length motion picture, the film is highly recommended for study of the Reformation.

3. "The Reformation," 16mm film, 52 minutes, color, 1967, NBC-TV, available from McGraw-Hill Films, 828 Custer Ave., Evans-

ton, IL 60202. Rental: $35.00. This is an objective film of the Reformation which covers the causes of church separation, the development of Protestantism, and much of the culture of the era. It is very good for discussion.

4. "The Story of the Christian Church," filmstrip, 50 frames, 1950. United Church of Christ, Office for Audio-Visuals, 1501 Race Street, Philadelphia, PA 19102. Sale: $3.00. This is a concise summary of church history with excellent artwork and good supplementary material.

5. "You Shall Be My Witness," filmstrip, 70 frames, color, script, guide, 1964. Graded Press, United Methodist Church, 201 Eighth Ave., S., Nashville, TN 37203. Also available from Cokesbury Bookstores. Sale: $4.25. Useful for a broad summary or general introduction to church history to stimulate further study, the film is easily divided into sections for viewing. Note that this is denominational publication.

D. Suggested Additional Case Studies

In the case study, "Augustine and the Mercy of God," by Ross Mackenzie, a famous Catholic theologian suggests how to teach ordinary people in the fifth century about God. He considers astrology a poor substitute for faith, questions whether the devil is real, and asks why Christ dies as a criminal on a cross. A deacon and teacher listening to Augustine struggles with what issues are most important at this moment in history.

The case, "Luther, Carlstadt, and Protestant Reform," by Louis Weeks, shows the famous sixteenth century reformer Martin Luther struggling with whether to return to his home church in Wittenberg to slow down what he sees as overzealous, destructive reforms at the church being made in his name. To return might not only endanger his own life but could again stir up riots in the town. However, if he does not return, his hopes for positive, slower changes in the church would surely fail.

These two historical cases are slightly longer and more complex than the other cases suggested, but are excellent for discussion and for enabling the participants to get in touch with the historical issues. Both cases can be found in *Case Studies in Christ and Salvation* (Philadelphia: Westminster, 1977), "Augustine," pp. 45–50 and "Luther," pp. 65–72, or they can be ordered separately from the Intercollegiate Case Clearing House, Soldier's Field, Boston, MA 02163.

E. Bibliography

Roland H. Bainton, *The Age of the Reformation*, (Princeton: Anvil Paperback, 1956). Combination of Reformation documents and commentary in a text form.

Roland H. Bainton, *Christendom*, 2 vols. (New York: Harper Torchbook, 1966). Excellent short history of Christianity and its impact on Western civilization, illustrated and written in a form appropriate for high school and college students. Bainton is one of the most readable scholars writing on the Reformation. Book deals with both Protestant and Roman Catholic reform.

Roland H. Bainton, *Here I Stand: A Life of Martin Luther* (New York: Apex & Mentor Paperbacks, 1951). Classic biography of Luther; basis for movie on Luther's life.

Marshall W. Baldwin, *The Mediaeval Church* (Ithaca, NY: Cornell, 1953). Provides a rapid glimpse of the Middle Ages and the role of the church.

George Brantl, ed., *Catholicism* (New York: Braziller, 1961). Basic interpretation of Catholic Christianity.

Robert McAfee Brown, *The Spirit of Protestantism* (New York: Oxford University Press, 1965). Basic interpretation of Protestant Christianity.

Tim Dowley, ed., *Eerdman's Handbook to the History of Christianity* (Grand Rapids: Eerdman's, 1977). Excellent, compact but thorough text.

Edwin Scott Gaustad, *A Religious History of America* (New York: Harper & Row, 1966). Good resource for suggested activity #3, see "The House," pp. 300–322.

Martin E. Marty, *Short History of Christianity* (Elnora, NY: Meridian Books, 1959). Precise, readable, and interesting history of Christianity.

Paul Tillich, *Christianity and the Encounter of the World Religions* (New York: Columbia University Press, 1963). Nature of religion and the question of mission discussed in a subtle and provocative way.

Timothy Ware, *Orthodox Church* (New York: Penguin, 1963). Good comprehensive introduction to the Orthodox Church from viewpoint of history, worship, doctrine, and church organization.

François Wendel, *Calvin* (New York: Harper & Row, 1963). Difficult reading, but excellent account of the origins and development of Calvin's religious thought.

RESOURCE GUIDE TO CASE STUDY C: "FREEDOM TO GROW"

1. ISSUES: First sort out the situation. Note that Mike was *driving* the car (and not *picked up* in the parking lot). Why were the Johnsons unhappy with Katie? With Mike? What decisions face Mary Johnson?

2. FEELINGS: Try next to discuss some of the feelings involved. List the five basic characters on the board (Mary, Katie and Bruce Johnson, Mike Fedson and Ted Mallory). Who seems angry and why? Is Katie afraid of what her mother may do? Is she concerned about the relationship to her peers? Is she being realistic? Work on how Mary Johnson *feels*. Does she care about Katie? What do you think about Bruce's role? How does Mike feel?

3. RESPONSIBILITY: Discuss what the word responsibility means. What were the various responsibilies of each of the five characters?

4. FREEDOM: How much freedom do Katie and Mike have? What can they do on their own? Does the law, enforced by the police, limit Mike's freedom? Is it responsible of the Johnsons to limit Katie's freedom? Discuss why or why not.

5. FAITH: Throughout this book, faith has been discussed as a relationship that implies trust and loyalty. What does it mean for Mary to have faith (trust) in Katie? (E.g., does she believe Katie's account of what happened?) Does this mean she should let Katie do whatever she wants to do?

6. LOVE: Does loving Katie mean that Mary must trust her in order for Katie to grow up? Why? Love as trust may depend on recognizing another person's worth and letting her or him make a decision even if it turns out later to be a mistake. However, love may involve protecting someone from making a mistake that may hurt them or others.
   How would Katie respond to these statements? How would Ka-

tie's father feel about this? Consider role playing Katie and her father discussing these two ideas for a few minutes.

7. HOPE: What do you think would be the most loving and trusting way for Katie's parents to respond to her? List as many alternatives as you can. Then discuss the *values* involved in the decisions each participant puts forward. What might change or transform Katie's future? Does she have any reasons for hope? How could the community of peers and parents be involved in the decision?

RESOURCE GUIDE TO CHAPTER 5

This chapter contains several concepts which may be difficult to grasp. Consider using these study questions as a basis for open discussion. Some possible ways to expand these questions are suggested below.

A. Study Questions

1. What does it mean to believe in someone? Think about various relationships you have with other people. What is the most trusting (dependable) relationship you have? Discuss why. What does a Christian mean by belief in, trust in, or faith in God? What kinds of experiences do Christians have to establish this relationship of faith? Some Christians would respond, a "change" in their lives, the witness of the scriptures and the history of the church, and the assurance of the present Christian community. What do these answers mean to you?

2. Discuss more fully the statement, "If one rightly understands what the Bible means by God as the Creator, he has rightly understood the whole Bible." What does the Christian understand is the intended relationship between the Creator and the creation (between God and humankind)? Do Christians feel they have any evidence that God seeks to maintain this relationship? (In your discussion, you may wish to consider the life and death of Jesus, God's gift of the Holy Spirit, the love persons show one another, and the "fullness of life" felt by many Christians.)

3. If God cares so much about people, why do terrible things such as murder, wars, famine, and acts of cruelty happen? Discuss three basic concepts of evil, and the freedom which God gives to humanity.

4. Think of the contexts in which you have used the word "sin." What does the word mean to you? What is the difference between a "sinful act" and "sin?" Some Christians find it helpful to discuss sin as separation from God. Can you think of times when concern for yourself (pride) made you *use* another person? In Christian terms, how does this "diminish" that other person's dignity or worth?

5. How would you distinguish between evil in the world and sin? Again, consider how you would define each of these terms. The United States is one of the wealthiest countries in the world, and yet each year thousands of people suffer from poor housing, an inadequate welfare system, and even malnutrition. Do you think this situation is due to evil or to sin? By "putting on the glasses of Christianity," could you argue a case for either side?

6. The notion that Christian practices are a result of Christian beliefs is crucial to an understanding of this chapter. Intentional actions are a result of commitments. Discuss why the practice of repentance is related to a particular understanding of God.

7. Following the original definition of a practice, apply this criteria to Christian prayer. Why do Christians pray? What does prayer "in Christ's name" imply for Christians? Why do you think the authors say that prayer, directly or indirectly, involves other people?

8. What does the word paradox mean? Christian paradoxes are some of the most difficult concepts to explain. Put into your own words the Christian idea of the Trinity. How can there be three and yet only one? Can you suggest another analogy for the Trinity besides the idea of a work of art?

9. Another Christian paradox is the concept of "free in Christ—servant to others." Study more carefully Galatians 5:13. When Paul refers to "slavery," do you think he is alluding both to the physical slavery of the Israelites in Egypt from which God freed them, and to their religious slavery to the Jewish laws? Why does Paul say a Christian isn't "justified by law," i.e., a recipient of salvation because he or she follows certain rules? If Christians then are free (do not have to "earn" salvation), why can't they do whatever they want? If someone lives wildly or irresponsibly, would Christians interpret this as true freedom or as being a "slave to self"? Why? Discuss this concept in relation to people who drink excessively and then drive an automobile. What are some of the basic criteria for a Christian to decide if certain actions express true freedom or license?

10. Discuss the concept of freedom in relation to the case study, "Freedom to Grow." Why does a growing child or teenager like

Katie need freedom? How does a growing person learn about herself and develop a sense of personal responsibility? How does this relate to the Christian understanding of why God has granted human freedom? Responsibility?

B. Suggested Projects and Activities

1. Research the "Freedom Rides" in the southern U.S. in the early 1960s (refer to dated copies of *Time, Newsweek*, etc.). Discuss what the word *freedom* means here. What was the position of churches who supported the rides? How would you explain the position of those who opposed the civil disturbances? Discuss how these different understandings reflect a difference in the Christian concept of freedom.

2. A current conflict in the Episcopal Church today is over the ordination of women. How do women interpret church positions which prohibit their serving as ordained ministers? What is the official position of the Episcopal Church on this issue? How does the church interpret the role of servant? Consider having two groups debate the issue, keeping in mind the theological issues involved.

3. Create a film or a number of posters on evil in the world, studying the aspects of human tragedy that surround us in the twentieth century. Then research and discuss the ways the Christian tradition has understood evil. What are the common elements in the variety of Christian interpretations?

C. Audio-Visual Materials

1. "The Antkeeper," (see information in Resource Guide to Chapter 1). This film offers discussion material for the concept of God the Creator and the relationship between God and humanity.

2. "Dancing Prophet," 16mm film, 15 minutes. Available from TeleKETICS, 1229 S. Santee St., Los Angeles, CA 90015. Rental: $15.00. A black American dancer living in Denmark communicates his faith through his lifework. The film is excellent for discussion of the unusual ways Christians can pray.

3. "The Greatest Madness of Them All," 16mm film, 28 minutes,

black and white, 1970, Paulist Productions. Available from Association Instructional Materials, 866 Third Avenue, New York, NY 10022. Rental: $10.00. A novelist deals with his own guilt and inability to allow forgiveness. This sophisticated film, recommended only for mature students, is good for an open discussion of the concepts of sin and forgiveness.

4. "Inscape," 16mm film, 30 minutes, color, 1968, National Council of Catholic Men. Available from Association Films, Inc. Rental: $15.00. Two teenagers discuss the painful problems which surround their lives and the world. The solution is open for discussion. Does Christianity have anything to say? The film is stimulating for a discussion of "the problem of evil."

5. "Night and Fog," 16mm film, 31 minutes, black and white, 1955, available from Contemporary/McGraw-Hill Films, Mass Media Ministries, 2116 N. Charles St., Baltimore, MD 21218 and many local film libraries. Rental: $30.00. This film for mature viewers only is a timeless, powerful record of the horrors of Nazi concentration camps, the inhumanity people display toward each other, the need for individual responsibility, and the concept of human freedom.

D. Bibliography

Martin Buber, *I and Thou* (New York: Scribner, 1970). Modern classic by a Jewish theologian on the relationship of love between persons. Has greatly influenced Christian views of community.

Mark Gibbard, *Why Pray?* (Valley Forge, PA: Judson, 1971). Good introduction to the subject of prayer and praying.

John Hick, *Evil and the God of Love* (Cleveland: Collins-World, 1974). Case study of evil from a historical and philosophical perspective.

John Macquarrie, *The Faith of the People of God* (New York: Scribner, 1973). A layperson's guide to theological concepts. Clearly written.

H. Richard Niebuhr, *The Meaning of Revelation* (New York: Macmillan, 1967). A modern classic on meaning of faith and how Christians understand God's self-revelation.

Reinhold Niebuhr, *The Nature and Destiny of Man*, 2 vols. (New York:

Scribner, 1949). Comprehensive and competent study of sin. A standard work on the relation between sin and freedom.

Frederick Sontag, *God, Why Did You Do That?* (Philadelphia: Westminster, 1970). A popular treatment of the problem of evil with a suggestive approach to an answer.

Paul Tillich, *Dynamics of Faith* (New York: Harper & Row Torchbook, 1957). Faith interpreted as being grasped by an ultimate concern.

Daniel D. Williams, *What Present-Day Theologians Are Thinking*, 3rd revised ed. (New York: Harper & Row Chapelbooks, 1967). Comprehensive reporting of major trends and movements in theology, both Protestant and Catholic. Written for the general reader.

RESOURCE GUIDE TO CHAPTER 6

A. Study Questions

1. How would you interpret the phrase "demand of love" in a Christian context? What did this mean for the Christian doctor? Was he forced to drink the flukes? Why or why not? Someone might say, "He would have been more loving to return to those people rather than risk dying and never going back." Do you agree? How would you interpret the doctor's motives for acting as he did?

2. How would you define "love" as described in the Bible? In your answer consider the example set by Christ, the parables you have read, what you know about the early church recorded in Acts, and the Old Testament image of God's faithfulness. Do you think that modern Christians are able to live up to these standards? Why or why not?

3. What do you understand as the basic criteria for making a decision from the Christian perspective? What happens when there is a conflict in these criteria? Christian love is an ideal. What happens when a Christian falls below this expectation?

4. How would you define morality? Ethics? What is the difference between morality and ethics? Are we basically a "moral" nation? Why or why not? Do you consider yourself a moral person?

5. Discuss the ways in which "Freedom to Grow" is a case dealing with ethics. What are the moral issues in the case that might require ethical reflection? (e.g., obeying the law, drinking and driving) Are the parents "social drinkers"? Do you think they ever drive after having a couple of beers? What peer pressure is there for Katie or her parents to drink? What values or criteria can someone use to resist peer pressure? Would your analysis of this case be any different if Mike had been picked up for possession of marijuana or hard drugs? Why or why not?

6. What are the *resources* for Christian ethics? Why do the authors say that ethics is not simply a "set of rules" for right conduct? Why would a Christian say that the practice of Christian ethics can lead to a more loving and fulfilling life? Might the resources

of the Christian faith help Katie and her parents in their ethical reflection and decision-making process? If so, how?

7. There are many good and loving people in the world who are not Christians. Why is the practice of Christian ethics not the same thing as Christianity? In what way could the response of a Christian to a situation be different from that of anyone else? Can the same action have different motives? Explain why or why not. What difference do the motives make?

8. How does Christian hope differ from "hoping it doesn't rain"? Consider how your expectations or dreams affect your present actions. This could be in the area of wanting to graduate from high school or college, wanting to be a musician, or even wanting a date on Saturday night.

9. How does the Christian concept of hope give meaning to the tremendous risk taken by the Christian doctor who drank the flukes? What might cause him to say it was hopeless and thus pour the flukes down the sink?

10. What does the Christian hope for? What do most Christians mean by "eternal life"? In what ways is eternal life a present as well as a future idea? How can a Christian's expectation of eternal life affect his or her present actions?

11. Why do most Christians not need *proof* of the resurrection of Christ? Study the words to some of the great Protestant Christian Easter hymns (e.g., "Christ the Lord Is Risen Today," first printed in London in 1739). Why is the resurrection important to a Christian?

12. How would you explain the concept of Christian peace to someone else? What sense does it make to say "peace is a gift"?

B. Suggested Activities and Projects

1. In order to discuss the definition of Christian love, divide into four small groups, each with one of the subheadings under love: rejoicing, gratitude, reverence, and loyalty. Participants could then consider carefully the modern definition of Christian love in this chapter and find examples in their daily lives to illustrate their section of the definition. Try to create a short skit which gives ex-

amples of these qualities of love, or summarize each group discussion for the rest of the class.

2. Read 1 Corinthians 13:1–13. This is Paul's classic definition of Christian love. Put this into your own words or give specific examples to illustrate what Paul means. Compare Paul's definition of love to the ones presented in this volume.

3. Interview members or religious leaders from different Christian churches (Roman Catholic, Orthodox, Methodist, Church of God, etc.) concerning what they mean by "eternal life" or "everlasting life." How does each think this affects what the members of their churches do in the present? Report back to the class with your own evaluations and responses to the interviews.

C. Suggested Audio-Visual Materials

1. "The Guest," 16mm film, 31 minutes, black and white, 1951. Twentieth Century-Fox. Available from Films, Inc., 5625 Hollywood Blvd., Hollywood, CA 90028. Rental: rates vary. This highly recommended film is about a shoemaker who waits for the Lord to visit him in his shop. "Technically superb, [this film] possesses a spirit of reverence and realism that places it among the finest religious materials ever produced." (Audio Visual Resource Guide)

2. "Let the Rain Settle It," 16mm film, 10 minutes, color, 1970, St. Francis Productions. Available from TeleKETICS, 1229 S. Santee St., Los Angeles, CA 90015. Rental: $10.00; super 8mm, rental: $9.00. Due to unforeseen circumstances a southern white boy must stay in the shack of a poor black family. The film deals with the power of God's love to overcome fear and hostility and the painful reality of the barriers humans place between individuals.

3. "Mother Waddles," 16mm film, 22 minutes, color, 1968, produced by Michael J. Kalush, 1101 Beard St., Flint, MI 48503. Apply for rental. This fascinating documentary is about an inner city black woman who is motivated by her understanding of Christian love to organize a variety of aid programs.

4. "The Red Kite," 16mm film, 17 minutes, color, 1967, National Film Board of Canada. Available from Augsburg Films, 426 S. Fifth St., Minneapolis, MN 55415 and numerous religious film

libraries. Rental: approx. $15.00. This sensitive, symbolic presentation of the concepts of love and death comes through the story of a father who helps his little girl fly a kite.

5. "A Year Towards Tomorrow," 16mm film, 28 minutes, (shorter version available—15 minutes), color, VISTA. Available from Sterling Films, 241 E. 34th St., New York, NY 10016. Three VISTA volunteers face rejection by the people they come to help. This is recommended for discussion of the nature of love for one's neighbor.

D. Suggested Additional Case Study

In the case study, "Carl Phillips Was Fired," the father of two teenage boys loses his job but does not tell his family for many months. Carl struggles with how he can deal with a sense of failure and how he can share his problems with others. Central issues in the case are vulnerability, risk, and the criteria for human worth. This case deals with one man's struggle to apply Christian love and to find hope in a difficult situation. The case and a study guide can be found in Louis and Carolyn Weeks and Robert and Alice Evans, *Casebook for Christian Living* (Atlanta: John Knox, 1977), pp. 66–86, or the case alone can be ordered directly from the Intercollegiate Case Clearing House, Soldier's Field, Boston, MA 02163.

E. Bibliography

Nicolas Berdyaev, *Freedom and the Spirit* (New York: Scribner, 1935). A classic consideration of love and freedom from a well known Orthodox theologian.

Joseph Fletcher, *Situation Ethics: The New Morality* (Philadelphia: Westminster, 1966). Controversial book which stresses the present situation as shaping ethical decisions.

Erich Fromm, *The Art of Loving* (New York: Harper & Row, 1974). Very well known psychological analysis of loving which sees it as a self-conscious, developed art.

James M. Gustafson & James T. Laney, eds., *On Being Responsible: Issues in Personal Ethics* (New York: Harper & Row, 1968). Selected essays on Christian ethics and its role in responsible decision-making.

James Moffatt, *Love in the New Testament* (London: Hadden & Stoughton, 1929). A classic analysis of love from the New Testament perspective. Out of print but found in religious section of most established libraries.

Jürgen Moltmann, *Theology of Hope* (New York: Harper & Row, 1967). Difficult but important book on the central role of hope in Christian belief.

H. Richard Niebuhr, *The Purpose of the Church and Its Ministry* (New York: Harper & Row, 1956). Relates the purpose of the church (increase of love of God and neighbor) to social ethics and ministry. Beautiful section on love, p. 34ff.

Jack L. Stotts, *Believing, Deciding, Acting* (Philadelphia: Geneva Press, 1968). Clear, interesting introduction to Christian ethics for the general reader with theme that personal response to biblical faith results in decision-making and action. Excellent for high school and college students.

Paul Tillich, *Love, Power and Justice* (New York: Oxford University Press, 1960). Concern for love when it takes seriously the need for power and the aim of justice.

Daniel D. Williams, *The Spirit and the Forms of Love* (New York: Harper & Row, 1968). Comprehensive review of the way the Bible, Christian tradition, and contemporary theology and philosophy view love. Difficult but rewarding.

RESOURCE GUIDE TO CASE STUDY D: "DANCE OF LIFE"

A. Teaching the Case

1. INTRODUCTION: After reading the case carefully, consider a warm-up exercise for this case. Play a piece of music like "I Wish I Knew What It Means to Be Free" (in the album: *The Gospel According to Don Shirley*, Columbia records). Close your eyes and imagine you are dancing to the music as Sara might wish to do. Note in the music a throb not unlike the noise a dialysis machine makes. After one or two minutes of this imaginary role, hold yourselves as if something were suddenly making it impossible to dance anymore. The author's class experience indicates that this exercise often makes an experiential contact with Sara's situation.

2. PERSONS: Remember that this is a real case, with real people who have strong feelings. What is the primary concern of each person in the case at this moment? Put one name on the board at a time (we suggest the order given below) and indicate the answers. Following are a sample of responses that a group might make.

Mrs. Graham (mother)
See Sara free of pain
"Can I face the loss?"
"If Sara dies, part of me dies."
Grief process needed
Pray for healing

Mr. Graham (father)
Sara, "hang-in there"
Terrible expense
Job relocation
Guilt
"O Lord, what did you do that for?"
"God's will be done!"

Dr. Adams (also family MD)
How to save Sara; responsibility
Ministry of health, wholeness
"God, don't let her die."
"No one dies voluntarily on me."

Mike (12)
"What is happening to me?"
"Sara will help me."
"If Sara can do it, I can."

Members of the Church
To have and to hold
How to be supportive of
  Graham family
Fear of having nothing to give
Uncertain how to minister

Pastor
Note his/her absence
Why? Priesthood of all believers
Develop role

Sara (16)	*Tracy (17)*
Needs Tracy's support	How to let go of one you love
Why suffer?	"Lord, help Thou my unbelief"
Death in life, life in death	How to deal with loss and anger
Healing—what is that?	How to love self
Lord of the Dance (resurrection)	Forgiveness
Giving in death	

3. ISSUES: What are some of the overall issues in the case?

a. *Quality of Life:* What does it mean for Sara to "live fully"? What are Sara's criteria for living a full life? What sense does it make to say, "Life is a gift of God and a Christian is charged to make the best of whatever life brings?" Consider the life of Helen Keller.

b. *Death and Dying:* How could Sara's death have some kind of meaning and dignity? Have you ever been close to anyone who was dying? If you know you are about to die, would it be better to do it in a hospital or at home? Why?

c. *Sacrifice:* Jesus said, "Greater love has no man than this, that a man lay down his life for his friends." (John 15:13 RSV) How much is Sara's decision influenced by her concern for Mike or her parents? If Sara decides to die, would you call it suicide or sacrifice for another?

d. *Eternal Life:* What do you think Sara means by "her assurance of a life after death"? Does eternal life begin only after you die? Would you interpret belief in eternal life as an escape from real life? Why or why not?

e. *Forgiveness and Community:* Would Tracy feel guilty if she supports Sara's decision and one year later a drug is discovered that makes transplants more successful? How can Tracy handle the possible loss of Sara and her own guilt? What can Mr. and Mrs. Graham or the community of friends do to help Sara? Should they try to get her to change her mind or support her decision? What would you do?

In the discussion of the issues you may want to try a brief role play between Sara and Tracy.

4. ALTERNATIVES: You might take a vote and see how many in the group think Sara should go home and die and how many think she should return to the hospital for dialysis and

continue to struggle? What are the alternatives for Sara and Tracy? They might look like this:

For Sara	For Tracy
Go home to die; how will she use the time?	Speak the truth about her feelings in love.
Delay decision; seek counsel and clarification.	Express her grief at the loss of Sara. Clarify the options for Sara.
Decide to live—change style of life.	Support Sara's decision in love. Resist Sara's decision in love.

Which alternative would you choose and why?

5. RESOURCES: To whom can the members of the Graham family turn for help? What resources are available to them? Do you think the members of their church might help? If so, how? If you were Tracy and you were going to pray, what would you pray for? Does the medical staff, persons like Dr. Adams, and the nurses, have any responsibility in this decision? Is Sara, herself, a resource to Tracy, her parents, or even herself? Will the decision made by the Grahams be any different because they are Christians?

Conclude the discussion by considering what major learnings have come out of a discussion of this case or of the earlier ones? Would you like to do more case studies in other courses? *Note:* Additional cases and an annotated bibliography on church-related cases may be ordered from the Intercollegiate Case Clearing House, Soldiers' Field, Boston, Mass. 02163.

B. Suggested Audio-Visual Materials

"Though I Walk Through the Valley," 30 minutes, 1973, color. Pyramid Films, P. O. Box 1048, Santa Monica, CA 90406. Rental: $25.00. Study guide provided free. This is an actual documentary of the last six months of a father with terminal cancer. His concept of death, shaped by Christian hope, strongly influences the relationship with his family. The film is the winner of the Council of International Non-Theatrical Events' Golden Eagle Award.

RESOURCE GUIDE TO CHAPTER 7

A. Study Questions

1. Discuss how Fred and Alice Thompson must have felt about the death of their daughter. Why did Fred want to find the student driver? Why do you think John Phillips could feel joyous at such a sad time?

2. Discuss how saying "good-bye" has become a ritual. What was the original meaning? What elements constitute a "ritual"? Do you have any ritual activities in your daily life? How do these rituals differ from religious rituals? What are some of the central Christian rituals?

3. What are the primary purposes of Christian worship? Why do the authors say that worship is "an attitude"? Discuss why worship for a Christian can take place outside of formal occasions. How do you think the symbolic actions of sacraments help the Christian to worship?

4. Discuss the concept of a symbol. A good example might be the U.S. flag. What kind of a response does the flag evoke? (E.g., memories of the battles for independence, Betsy Ross, idea of freedom, etc.) Some of the Christian symbols are water, bread, and wine. What does water symbolize for the Christian?

5. What is the ritual of baptism about? What "rite of passage" does it mark in the life of a believer? What event does it remember in Christ's life? Why do some Christians put on new clothes after baptism? Why is the baptismal basin or font located in a prominent place in most churches?

6. What step in a Christian's life is marked by confirmation? How can this be compared to an initiation ritual? Discuss the biblical scripture (Acts 8:14–17) cited as the origin of the ritual of confirmation. Why do some Christians combine confirmation and baptism?

7. You may wish to review the section on repentance in Chapter 5 as a prelude to the discussion of penance. Why must this ritual be repeated by Christians? Why do Christians believe God will continue to forgive them? Someone has said that confession

before Communion or the Eucharist can be compared to washing your hands before a meal. What does this analogy mean?

8. Why would many Christians consider the ritual of Communion or the Lord's Supper the most central symbolic action of the faith? How would you compare this "meal" with the Jewish passover meal? Discuss why Communion is a unifying ritual for diverse groups of Christians. Why do some Christian churches have very strict rules about who can take Communion?

9. Discuss why the rituals of marriage and ordination are "rites of passage." What new responsibilities do the participants assume? What does the ring symbolize in a Christian marriage? What does the "laying on of hands" symbolize in the ordination of a pastor?

10. Discuss the way in which a Christian funeral is a drama. What aspects of Christ's life does the drama relive? Why can a funeral be a time of celebration for a Christian?

11. How do you feel about the case of Sara Graham? Do you understand her decision? Do you think she made the wrong decision? Why or why not?

12. You may know the tune to "Lord of the Dance." Sing the tune or bring a recording. Discuss the symbols of dancing. Try to fill in the events of each stanza. What do you think this song communicates about the Christian concept of eternal life?

B. Suggested Activities and Projects

1. Of necessity this chapter dealt only briefly with each sacrament. The various rituals could provide interesting, individual research topics. Groups or individuals could report to the class and perhaps show slides or pictures of how a particular Christian tradition celebrates each sacrament. As the church traditions of marriage, Communion (Eucharist), baptism, and confession vary considerably, keep in mind the core elements common to these rituals.

2. Visit a number of different worship services. How are they different? How do you think these differences developed? How are they alike? Again, keep a list of the common factors in most forms of Christian worship.

3. Death is a fact of life many American cultural patterns seek to ignore. See Jessica Mitford's controversial book *The American Way of Death*, (New York: Simon & Schuster, 1963). Discuss the way a funeral is conducted and who helps the family to deal with their loss. The basis of the discussion could be an interview with a pastor, an advisor in a family counseling center, a mortician (funeral director), or a representative of a Christian burial society (groups organized to assist families and reduce the high cost of burial or cremation). Do Christian organizations respond any differently than others to the question of death?

C. Audio-Visual Suggestions

1. "Baptism—The Sacrament of Resurrection," sound filmstrip, 15 minutes, color, 1967. Available from Thomas S. Klise, Co., P. O. Box 3418, Peoria, IL 61614. Sale: $16.50. This film explores the meaning of baptism as "new life" and deals with the concept of fullness of life.

2. "Death of a Peasant," 16mm film, 10 minutes, color. Available from International Film Bureau, 332 S. Michigan Ave., Chicago, IL 60609. Rental: $15.00. The love story of a Yugoslav peasant who chooses death by his own hands over a German firing squad. The film is a courageous self-assertion of individual integrity. "A truly magnificent film leading to innumerable areas of discussion, especially on questions of free will, self-determination, and death." (Wavelength Newsletter, published by the National Humanities Faculty)

3. "Eucharist" or "Holy Communion" (Same film—two titles), 16mm film, 10 minutes, color, 1969. Available from TeleKET-ICS, 1229 S. Santee St., Los Angeles, CA 90015. Rental: $10.00; super 8mm, rental: $9.00. This film, which combines scenes of the sacrament along with everyday scenes of life—work, joy, suffering —is good for discussion of the meaning of Communion for the Christian.

4. "Penance: Sacrament of Peace," 16mm film, 10 minutes, color, 1969. TeleKETICS. Rental: $10.00; super 8mm, rental: $9.00. This well-made film is about a young man who accidentally paralyzes a child and his dealing with his own guilt feelings. It is excel-

lent for discussion of the dangers of drinking when driving, the role of penance, and the significance of forgiveness.

5. "Sacrament of Belonging," 16mm film, 10 minutes, color, 1969, St. Francis Productions. Available from TeleKETICS. Rental: $10.00; super 8mm, rental: $9.00. This moving, highly sensitive film about a homeless, disfigured boy searching for acceptance, symbolically portrays the meaning of baptism. It is a powerful film.

6. "The Supper," 16mm film, 20 minutes, black and white, 1967. Paul F. Keller and Asso. Available from Augsburg Films, 426 S. Fifth St., Minneapolis, MN 55415. Rental: $20.00. This symbolic story of a fisherman and a man in a tent is quite provocative for a discussion of human relations, Christian love, forgiveness, and the implications of the Lord's Supper or Eucharist.

D. Bibliography

Walter H. Abbott, S. J., ed., *The Documents of Vatican II* (New York: Association Press, 1966). See especially "Constitution on the Sacred Liturgy" which is the official Roman Catholic position on worship and sacrament with concern for "indigenization" of the Mass in different cultures.

George M. Gibson, *The Story of the Christian Year* (New York: Abingdon, 1951). A study of the pagan and Christian origin of the Christian liturgical calendar. Found in religious libraries.

Elizabeth Kübler-Ross, *On Death and Dying* (New York: Macmillan, 1969). Classic work on understanding and counseling those who are dying.

Robert Neale, *The Art of Dying* (New York: Harper & Row, 1973). Written by a professor of Psychiatry and Religion out of experience of a year in a hospital for the terminally ill. Has imaginative exercises to help a person face his or her own death and understand the Christian language of death and resurrection.

Geoffrey Parrinder, *Worship in the World's Religions* (New York: Association Press, 1961). Can be found in many libraries. Good, clear description of Christian patterns of celebration pp. 206–231.

Evelyn Underhill, *Worship* (New York: Harper & Row, 1973). Classic study of worship (like her work on *Mysticism*) with a helpful survey of ways of worship in main branches of Christianity today. Found in theological libraries.

Granger E. Westberg, *Good Grief* (Philadelphia: Fortress, 1962). Very readable little book on the ten stages of grief persons go through in any loss, but particularly that of death. Practical book for Christians in the grief process.

James F. White, *New Forms of Worship* (Nashville: Abingdon, 1971). Contemporary examination of worship, its meaning, and innovative forms from the Protestant perspective.

RESOURCE GUIDE TO CHAPTER 8

This chapter can be used to help pull together learnings about Christianity.

A. Study Questions

1. Discuss the first story in Chapter 8 about the father and his three children. Why do the authors say that making a commitment to a certain religious tradition involves risk? What kind of risk?

2. At this stage of the study are you any clearer about your own ultimate concern? From what perspective do you understand the reality of human life in the world?

3. Do you feel a religious tradition can remain strong if there are different ways of worshiping and understanding? If there is disagreement on this in your group, consider a debate between two groups who have been given the time outside class to develop their ideas as teams.

4. What do you now see as the core elements of Christianity which are common to almost all of the Christian groups? Trace these elements back through the preceding chapters.

B. Suggested Activities and Projects

1. Draw a *picture* of the unit on Christianity. What is your own symbolic representation of this religion? You may want to interpret your drawing for others.

2. Consider interviewing pastors or laypersons in local Protestant, Roman Catholic, and Eastern Orthodox churches to learn how their members celebrate Holy Week. You might also study the parallel patterns of worship during Advent, Christmas, and Epiphany. What factors in the diverse culture of America may have influenced these patterns of celebration? A sub-report might deal with the origin of the Easter egg and the European practice of painting eggs. Similarly, with the Christmas season, a group might investigate the origin of Santa Claus or Father Christmas. Has commercialism influenced these celebrations in America? Respond to the reports on the various patterns of the same cele-

bration in America by drawing out the core elements common to all of the celebrations.

3. Research the various means of evangelism in your own community. Be sure and use the broader use of this term, meaning not only to share the "good news" in words, but also in service to others. Consider "revivals" but also investigate Christian day-care centers, nursing homes, etc. Consider interviewing some of the leaders of these institutions about how they see their role in "sharing the gospel."

4. Try a role play between two students, one representing a person from another planet and the other representing him or herself. Ask the second student to try to explain what a religion is and what this particular religion called Christianity is about. Your "person from another planet" should be sure to ask questions if the speaker depends on "common knowledge" or preconceptions about Christianity.

C. Audio-Visual Materials

1. "Roadsigns on a Merry-go-round," 16mm film, 27 minutes, color. Available from Marlin Motion Pictures, 47 Lakeshore Road E., Port Credit, Ontario, Canada. This is an interesting film to use in summary of the Christianity unit. It explores personal responses to the meaning of life and contains an introduction to the philosophies of Tielhard de Chardin, Martin Buber, and Dietrich Bonhoeffer.

2. Consider using one of the general "Christianity" films or filmstrips such as the *Life* series to help summarize the basic concepts of Christianity [cited in the General Bibliography].

D. Bibliography

American Catholicism, by John T. Ellis, 1969.

American Judaism, by Nathan Glazier, 1972.

American Protestantism, by Wintrop S. Hudson, 1961. These three books by the University of Chicago Press are sometimes called the "Chicago Trilogy." They provide a summary of the three major religious traditions and illustrate the variety of expressions and interrelationship between the three in the United States.

Dietrich Bonhoeffer, *Letters and Papers from Prison* (New York: Macmillan, 1972) and *The Cost of Discipleship* (New York: Macmillan, 1967). Written by a famous German theologian who was executed in a Nazi concentration camp for actively resisting the Nazi attempt to exterminate the Jews and for involvement in a plot to assassinate Hitler. Illustration of the risk commitment to Christianity may involve.

Edwin Scott Gaustad, *A Religious History of America* (New York: Harper & Row, 1966). Contains illustrations and an informative text on the concepts of Mission and Evangelism in the U.S. and abroad, pp. 324–371. Also has interesting sections on Christian beliefs and patterns of worship, pp. 271–284 and pp. 285–305.

Henry P. Van Dusen, *World Christianity: Yesterday - Today - Tomorrow* (New York: Abingdon Press, 1947). Standard introduction to ecumenical movement by one of its most prominent spokesmen. Found in most religious libraries, it gives a picture of the world-wide presence of Christianity.

ANNOTATED GENERAL BIBLIOGRAPHY

Books listed here are basic resources applicable to the entire volume. The more focused bibliographies that follow the study suggestions for each chapter sometimes refer to a specific section of a book named in this General Bibliography.

General Reference:

The Editors of Life, *The World's Great Religions* (New York: Time, Inc., 1963). An excellent source for pictures relevant to all major religions. Christianity section pp. 163–305.

Life Education Program. The six-part series on religion, originally part of *Life* magazine, is now available in reprint form. The series is characterized by colorful illustrations and concise comment. A series of six filmstrips (each with its own lecture booklet) corresponding to the six reprints is also available. Christianity is Part VI. For full information write to Life Education Program, Box 834, Radio City Post Office, New York, New York 10019.

Allan Evans, Riley Moynes, Larry Mortinello, *What Man Believes* (Toronto: McGraw-Hill, 1973). Prepared for a high school reading level, has a glossary, maps, charts, and bibliography.

John B. Noss, *Man's Religions*, 5th edition (New York: Macmillan, 1974). One of the better detailed studies of the history of religions for the general reader and scholar.

Geoffrey Parrinder, *The Faiths of Mankind: A Guide to the World's Living Religions* (New York: Thomas Crowell, 1965). Very brief, concise picture of Christianity with an interesting comparison of Christian practices of worship.

Ninian Smart, *The Religious Experience of Mankind* (New York: Scribner, 1969). An innovative study of comparative religion.

Huston Smith, *The Religions of Man* (New York: Harper & Row, 1958). Contains a beautifully written, brief picture of Christianity.

Definition of Christian Terms:

Marvin Halverson, ed., *Handbook of Christian Theology* (New York: Meridian Books, 1960).

Alan Richardson, *A Dictionary of Christian Theology* (Philadelphia: West-minster, 1969).

Audio-Visual References:

Nick Abrams, ed., *Audio-Visual Resource Guide,* 9th edition, (New York: Friendship Press, 1972). This seems to be the most complete evalua-tive guide on available Christian audio-visual materials. It provides fuller information on most films and filmstrips recommended in this guide. In locating any of the films recommended, before writing to the distributor, first contact religious film libraries, public libraries, and denominational church libraries in your area. The rental fees listed in this guide represent the average charge, as the fee varies with different libraries.

Thousands of additional films have been produced each year since the publication of the *Audio-Visual Resource Guide.* For a wide selection of the most recent theological-ethical films, write to the following distribu-tors for their catalogs:

Films Inc. The largest source of current and classic theatrical films available in 16mm. 5625 Hollywood Blvd., Hollywood, CA 90028.

Pyramid Films Producers, Inc. The most comprehensive source of short, experimental animated, educational, and discussion-starting films in 16mm and videotape. Box 1048, Santa Monica, CA 90406.

Paulist Productions. Catholic producer of the INSIGHT series, 30-min-ute dramatized cases using award-winning writers and directors. 17575 Pacific Coast Highway, Pacific Palisades, CA 90272.

Franciscan Communication Center. Producer of the TeleKETIC films and spots. 1229 Santee St., Los Angeles, CA 90015.

Mass Media Ministries. An excellent collection of theological and ethi-cal films gathered from many different producers. 2116 N. Charles St., Baltimore, MD 21218.

Gospel Films, Inc. The largest collection of evangelical fundamentalist produced films, with some appropriate documentaries and filmed case studies. Box 455, Muskegon, MI 49443.

National Film Board of Canada. Exceptional films with many case study documentaries. 1251 Avenue of the Americas, New York, NY 10020.

Basic Bible Course for Schools. Frequently, a special problem in teaching

Christianity is that most people lack sufficient content knowledge of the Bible. One unusual and creative approach to meet this need is the Basic Bible Course for Schools. The course includes eight audio cassettes which give an overview of each of the sixty-six books of the Protestant/Orthodox Old and New Testament. The system coordinates with a workbook. One book of the Bible can be covered in about six minutes or the whole Bible can be reviewed in about eight hours. The material presents a concise review of the Bible in non-technical and non-interpretive language.

Prepared by a seminary instructor of communications and a producer of Christian radio and TV programs, the tapes are designed for use by one person or a group. Cost ranges from $5.00 to $69.00 depending on number of tapes and workbooks ordered. There is also an excellent set of four cassette tapes and a workbook on Church History from the early church to the Reformation.

For information on both series contact Contemporary Catacombs, 2637 N. Mildred, Chicago, Illinois 60614.

Resources for Religion Studies. Ontario Dept. of Education. Available free of charge from Public Education Religion Studies Center, Wright State Univ., Dayton, Ohio 45431. Contains annotated list of Bibliography, Films, Filmstrips, Reprints, Recordings of Sacred Music, and Replicas.

Additional Casebooks:

Robert and Alice Evans and Carolyn and Louis Weeks, *Casebook for Christian Living: Value Formation for Families and Congregations,* (Atlanta: John Knox, 1977). Contains twelve case studies with study guides for each. Text deals with how central Christian concepts influence the formation of personal values. Designed for use by church-oriented groups. Contains an appendix on case teaching.

Robert A. Evans and Thomas D. Parker, eds., *Christian Theology: A Case Method Approach* (New York: Harper & Row, 1976) Thirty-six Christian theologians representing varying theological perspectives respond to nine cases. Cases and responses highlight major doctrines in the Apostles' Creed.